THE COMPLETE HUNTER™

THE COMPLETE GUIDE TO
HUNTING

Basic Techniques for Gun & Bow Hunters

Gary Lewis

Creative Publishing
international

Minneapolis, Minnesota

Gary Lewis *is an outdoor writer, speaker and photographer. He has hunted and fished in five countries on two continents and much of the American West. He is a past President of the* Northwest Outdoor Writers Association (NOWA) *and is Associate Editor for* Hunting the West *magazine. Lewis is the author or co-author of seven books, including Creative Publishing International's* Black Bear Hunting *with Lee Van Tassell. Four of his books have won NOWA's Excellence in Craft awards and he has received numerous awards for his newspaper columns and magazine articles. His stories have appeared in many prestigious outdoor magazines such as* Sports Afield, Rifle, Successful Hunter, African Sporting Gazette *and* Traditional Bowhunter. *He lives in Bend, Oregon.*

Creative Publishing
international

Copyright © 2008
Creative Publishing international, Inc.
400 First Avenue North
Suite 300
Minneapolis, MN 55401
Chanhassen, Minnesota 55317
1-800-328-0590
www.creativepub.com

President/CEO: Ken Fund
VP/Sales & Marketing: Kevin Hamric
Publisher: Bryan Trandem
Acquisition Editor: Barbara Harold
Production Managers: Laura Hokkanen, Linda Halls

Creative Director: Michele Lanci-Altomare
Senior Design Managers: Brad Springer, Jon Simpson
Design Managers: Sara Holle, James Kegley
Book & Cover Design: Danielle Smith
Page Layout: Danielle Smith

Contributing Photographers: Phil Aarrestad, Grady Allen, Charles Alsheimer, Erwin Bauer, Craig Blacklock, Les Blacklock, Tom Brakefield, Browning, Glenn D. Chambers, Tim Christie, Herbert Clarke, Daniel J. Cox, Gary Kramer, John Ebeling, Michael Francis, Michael Furtman, Eric J. Hansen, Larry D. Jones, Gary Kramer, Lon E. Lauber, Gary Lewis, Tom Mangelson, Bill Marchel, Tom Martinson, Jay Massey, Worth Mathewson, Bill McRae, Wyman Meinzer, Arthur Morris/Birds as Art, William H. Mullins, Doug Murphy, Scott Nielsen, Jerome B. Robinson, Lynn Rogers, Leonard Lee Rue, III, Dwight R. Schuh, Ron Shade, Jerry Smith, Dale C. Spartas, Ron Spomer, Norm Strung, Syl Strung, Ken Thommes, Charles Waterman, Chuck Wechsler, Ron Winch, James Zacks, Gary Zahm
Contributing Illustrator: Jon Q. Wright

Library of Congress Cataloging-in-Publication Data
Lewis, Gary
 The complete guide to hunting : basic techniques for gun and bow hunters / Gary Lewis.
 p. cm.
 ISBN-13: 978-1-58923-373-7 (hard cover)
 ISBN-10: 1-58923-373-5 (hard cover)
 1. Hunting. I. Title.
 SK33.L49 2008
 799.2--dc22   2007033514

Printed in China

10 9 8 7 6 5 4 3 2 1

CONTENTS

INTRODUCTION

Whether the hunt takes you after Rocky Mountain elk along the western skyline or into a Carolina swamp behind a pack of beagles, the chase offers a unique challenge. Rabbit, deer, elk, moose or bear, whatever the quarry, the hunter must outsmart a wild animal with a better knowledge of its environment and keener senses.

This challenge, along with the camaraderie of the hunt, accounts for the sport's tremendous popularity. And a successful hunter can enjoy a year-round supply of lean, nutritious meat.

The Complete Guide to Hunting is intended to make the reader a better hunter. Each section of the book deals with a different facet of the sport. Together, they will help you develop the skills and savvy needed to consistently bag wild game.

The first chapter, "All About Wild Game," provides an understanding of wildlife behavior and helps you recognize good habitat. By knowing how animals sense danger, react to threats and find food, water and cover, you can improve your chances of being in the right spot at the right time.

Chapter 2, "Hunting Skills and Equipment," provides all the information needed to select rifles, shotguns, bows and muzzleloaders. Learn how to choose the best ammunition for the game and how to become a proficient shooter. This chapter goes far beyond the basics, explaining complex principles of bullet and shot performance with descriptive photos and easy-to-understand charts.

The third chapter, "Hunting Strategies," teaches how to plan the hunt and how to scout a potential spot to make sure it holds game. This chapter details the most popular hunting techniques, from stalking to driving. Learn how to tailor a hunting strategy to the terrain and time of day. It also provides valuable tips for recovering game.

The final four chapters acquaint you with North America's most popular game animals. Hundreds of informative how-to photos, along with a fact-filled text, give all the information needed to locate, pursue and bag each of these species.

Astounding photography puts you in the scene. Face-off with a huge bull moose; walk a fencerow and see a ring-necked pheasant burst from cover at your feet; experience the nerve-wracking anticipation of waiting for a wild turkey to strut close enough for a shot.

The hunting techniques found in this book are those considered most effective by the nation's top hunting authorities. Hunting regulations and legal equipment differ in every state and province, so it is possible that some of the procedures described are illegal in your area. Baiting bears, for instance, is a popular method in some states, but is against the law in others. Check the local hunting laws before going afield.

In addition to the proven high-percentage hunting methods, this book also reveals dozens of little-known but effective tips that help the experts take their game. You will learn how to attract diving ducks by waving a black flag and how to imitate a scolding squirrel by clicking quarters.

This book is a unique blend of straightforward writing and captivating photography. Never before has so much how-to hunting information and so many dramatic wildlife photographs been packed into one volume. *The Complete Guide to Hunting* is sure to make your days afield more enjoyable—and more successful.

Chapter 1

ALL ABOUT WILD GAME

From the moment of birth, a game animal faces threats from predators, weather, disease and competition. Only the strongest and wariest live long enough to reproduce. In this way, nature selects the best breeding stock to ensure that the species thrives.

All game animals have the potential to produce many more offspring than the habitat can support. Reproductive rates are high among small game and upland birds. High mortality rates are nature's way of keeping game populations in check. When too many animals survive, the population explosion causes disease, stunted growth and eventually starvation.

Among most upland birds, waterfowl and small game, 60 to 80 percent of the population dies each year. Individuals over one year old comprise only 20 to 40 percent of the fall population. Because young animals are more abundant and because they lack the savvy of older animals, they make up the bulk of the hunter's bag.

Regulations are based on the concept that game can be harvested as long as breeding stock remains to produce another crop of similar size the following year. Seasons for small game, waterfowl and upland birds are usually long and bag limits generous. Liberal regulations are possible because of the high reproductive rates of these animals. Regulations for big game are stricter because the animals produce fewer young.

Resource agencies monitor game populations and set regulations to achieve the desired harvest. Scientific wildlife management has eliminated the problems of mass slaughter associated with market hunting in years past. In fact, some of the continent's most popular game species, such as white-tailed deer and wild turkey, are more numerous today than at any time in recorded history.

THREE SENSES

Game animals have an amazing ability to elude hunters. Their keen senses of sight, smell and hearing enable them to detect danger far in advance and take evasive action. Many animals also possess unique survival adaptations that far exceed the capabilities of humans.

SIGHT. Game birds have color vision that may surpass that of humans. Their retinas have more color receptors, or cones, than most other game animals. Colored oil droplets in the retina work like a camera filter, enhancing the visibility of certain hues. The cones also give them excellent visual acuity, or sharpness.

Game mammals have retinas that contain mostly light receptors, or rods. The rods enable them to see well in dim light. The vision of most game mammals is not as sharp as that of birds or humans and they have limited color vision, if any.

Most mammals have poor accommodation capabilities; they cannot change the shape of their lenses to focus on both close and distant objects. As a result, images are often fuzzy. This explains why many types of big game animals do not seem to notice a stationary hunter.

SMELL. Game mammals collect most of the information about their environment through their sense of smell. In a laboratory test, rabbits were able to detect the smell of acetone at a concentration of only 1/50 of that detectable by humans. Hunters who pursue big or small game should try to approach from downwind to keep their scent from drifting toward the animals.

Game birds have a poor sense of smell. In one study, wild turkey were given two piles of grain, one of which contained a highly repulsive scent. The birds paid no attention to the odor, feeding equally at each pile. To a bird in flight, a highly-developed sense of smell would be of little value because odors produced by predators quickly sink to the ground.

HEARING. Because game birds lack external ears and because their ears have fewer small bones than those of mammals, they are not as well equipped for detecting faint sounds. The range of pitches they can recognize is slightly less than that of humans and substantially less than that of many game mammals.

In a test of their ability to detect various pitches, mallards recognized sounds up to a frequency of 8,000 cycles per second (cps). Humans detected higher pitched

FACTORS THAT AFFECT GAME POPULATIONS

Big game populations can reach high levels despite low reproductive rates. Predators take only an occasional young animal. In areas with good habitat and little hunting pressure, herds may grow so large that food shortages result. Hunting regulations are set to control the harvest, yet prevent overpopulation.

Game populations tend to remain stable if the habitat is not disturbed and hunting pressure is regulated. In a study of a ruffed grouse population in New York state, there were 174 adult grouse at the beginning of the breeding season. These birds produced 935 fertile eggs. As the months passed, 24 adult grouse succumbed to predators and disease, 26 to hunting and 54 to severe weather. By the following spring, 70 birds remained to breed again. Of the 935 eggs, 374 were destroyed by predators. The rest hatched, but 337 chicks were killed by predators and disease. Hunters claimed 38 of the young birds, 81 perished in winter storms and 105 survived to the breeding season. These first-year breeders, combined with the 70 second-year birds, resulted in a total of 175 adult grouse, nearly identical to the breeding population of the previous year.

sounds, up to 20,000 cps and raccoon heard sounds of up to 85,000 cps.

SPECIAL ADAPTATIONS. The process of evolution has provided almost every species of game animal with some unique physical feature or ability that gives it an advantage over other animals. These adaptations enable the species to survive the threats posed by predators, including humans.

Many of these adaptations are so foreign to humans that we fail to consider them when hunting.

For example, a mallard can stay submerged for as long as 16 minutes. It accomplishes this seemingly impossible feat by slowing its heart rate by more than 50 percent while underwater. This substantially reduces its oxygen needs.

Many a hunter has winged a duck, marked it down, spent 5 to 10 minutes looking for it, then given up in frustration. After the hunter returns to the blind, the live duck reappears in the very spot it went down.

Hunters who understand the senses and special adaptations of the game they pursue stand the best chance of success.

COMPARING HUMAN AND GAME SENSES

	Vision	Hearing	Smell
Human	*Good*	*Good*	*Fair*
White-tailed Deer	*Fair*	*Excellent*	*Excellent*
Cottontail Rabbit	*Good*	*Excellent*	*Good*
Wild Turkey	*Excellent*	*Excellent*	*Poor*
Ring-necked Pheasant	*Good*	*Good*	*Poor*
Mallard duck	*Excellent*	*Good*	*Fair*

Color vision exists in some big game. In one study, white-tailed deer were rewarded with a drink from a tube when a red light went on; a white light gave no reward. Even though the lights switched between two tubes, deer consistently made the right choice.

Night vision in nocturnal animals is enhanced by the tapetum lucidum, a layer of reflective pigment below the surface of the retina. Light passes through the receptors on the retina's surface, hits the tapetum, then bounces back to stimulate the receptors again.

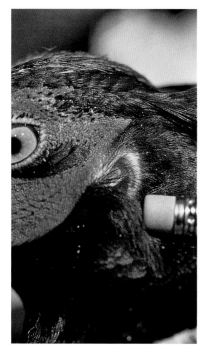

Internal ears of birds do not collect sounds as efficiently as exposed ears. And because the ears are close together, they are not as well suited to locating the direction of sounds.

Exposed ears gather sound waves. They also help an animal pinpoint the source of a sound by the difference in the time it takes for the signal to reach each ear.

Movable ears enable mammals to locate sounds from any direction. While one ear detects a sound from one direction, the other picks up a sound from a different source.

Positioning themselves below the crest of a wind-swept ridge enables some big game to smell anything approaching from above. They watch for anything coming from below. Scent glands warn other animals of danger. When a mule deer faces a threat, metatarsal glands on the hind legs produce an odor that alerts other herd members.

Freezing in position and pressing its body to the ground (right) reduces the amount of scent an animal gives off. Some game birds also compress their feathers so less scent escapes.

OTHER SPECIAL ADAPTATIONS

Flared rump hair alerts other animals to a threat. By flaring its rump hairs to the side, the pronghorn can greatly increase the size and visibility of its white rump patch.

Camouflage enables game animals to escape detection by predators. The woodcock, for example, blends in so well with the vegetation that it can hide in open terrain with no overhead cover.

Genetic changes may result from hunting. The tendency to run has increased among pheasants. Many hunters attribute this to the fact that fliers get shot, leaving runners to breed.

WILDLIFE HABITAT

The best wildlife environment has a variety of plant life that provides food and cover. A mixed plant community generally supports more species and higher numbers of game than an expanse of the same type of vegetation.

Good habitat is the key to an abundant wildlife population. To survive and thrive, a game animal needs food, shelter cover, room to escape and water. A reliable supply of drinking water is important, although some animals find sufficient moisture in their foods.

Most game species find the necessary plant variety along the edge between two vegetative types. Where a forest meets a marsh, for instance, the mixture of grasses, berry bushes, low-growing leafy plants and young trees provide an excellent supply of food and cover. The area where the two types of vegetation meet usually holds more kinds and higher numbers of game than either type by itself. Hunters call this "edge habitat."

Another factor that influences plant variety is succession. For example, after a forest fire or logging operation, the bare ground almost immediately begins to grow grasses, shrubs and trees. As the trees grow taller, they form a canopy that shades the forest floor. As the canopy grows denser, shrubs and grasses disappear because of the lack of sunlight. Eventually, only large trees remain. These changes in the plant community invariably affect the type and amount of game the habitat can support.

Succession begins after trees have been removed. New grasses, shrubs and trees support animals like white-tailed deer. As time goes on, trees grow taller, yet enough sunlight penetrates to promote a dense growth of underbrush ideal for animals like ruffed grouse. As the trees mature and shade the forest floor, underbrush disappears and the forest becomes best suited for animals like black bear.

Wildlife managers often set back the process of succession by periodically cutting or burning forested areas to promote growth of new vegetation. These techniques enable them to increase the production of important game species.

In most agricultural areas, the trend is toward less habitat variety. Many farms once had small, weedy crop fields combined with brushy fence lines, unmowed roadside ditches, large wetlands and dense groves. Today's clean farms have vast acreages of crops unbroken by fence lines, wetlands or trees. Even roadside ditches are often mowed for hay. These intensive agricultural practices severely reduce or eliminate populations of farmland game like pheasants and quail.

Cover Requirements

Escape cover is vital to the survival of almost every game species. Wildlife also needs other kinds of cover for bedding, loafing, protection from the elements and producing young.

A ring-necked pheasant, for example, often escapes from hunters by hiding in dense brush. It may roost in open grasslands, loaf along the grassy margin of a crop field and burrow under a clump of slough grass during a storm. Experienced hunters know where to look at different times of the day and under different weather conditions.

ESCAPE COVER. Predators pose a constant threat to most game animals. Wildlife must learn to contend with these threats or perish. Most elude predators by hiding in dense cover; others scamper to a burrow or den; in light cover, some crouch motionless or rely on camouflage.

BEDDING COVER. Some game animals bed in dens or burrows or roost in trees. Others prefer thick grassy cover for bedding sites. The grass offers concealment and warns animals of danger. Even the stealthiest predator finds it difficult to move through thick grass without making some noise.

Adequate shelter cover is crucial to ensure winter survival. Bobwhite quail roost on the ground to exchange body heat. They may be found in low-growing cover on agricultural lands and around farm equipment on old homesteads.

WHERE TO FIND EDGE HABITAT

Forest clearings, like powerline corridors, logging roads and logged or burned areas, usually hold more game than the forest interior. Marshes or grassy meadows in the forests also attract wildlife.

Farmlands abutting forests or brushlands have an abundance of edge habitat. Ample sunlight reaches the forest or brushland margin, resulting in a lush growth of seed- and berry-producing plants.

Mountain slopes often have edge habitat where grassy foothills meet mid-elevation hardwoods; where hardwoods grade into high-elevation conifers; and at the treeline, where conifers end and lichens begin.

LOAFING COVER. Most game animals feed in early morning and late afternoon, then loaf during mid day. Loafing cover is thick enough so that animals are not easily visible, but not so dense that they cannot see.

COVER FROM THE ELEMENTS. All game animals need some type of dense cover to insulate them from extremely cold temperatures. They also use cover as shelter from precipitation, strong winds and the hot summer sun.

Many birds and small mammals crawl under vegetation to escape harsh winter storms. Some burrow under the snow, creating a cozy enclosure. The animal's body heat may keep the temperature as much as 50 degrees warmer than the outside air. Big game animals may bed under conifer limbs in a heavy rain or on a cold night. The boughs shed precipitation and act like a blanket to slow the loss of body heat into the atmosphere.

Abandoned buildings serve as windbreaks for many types of game. Old farmsteads often have discarded machinery, brush piles, tall weeds and evergreen groves that offer cover from the elements.

PRODUCTION COVER. Predators and adverse weather quickly wipe out nesting adults and newly produced young unless they have good production cover. This type of cover may not hold animals during the hunting season, but it often serves as an indicator of high game populations.

BASIC COVER TYPES

Open timber (left) is used as loafing cover by some types of big game. Small game and upland birds generally loaf in areas with denser ground cover.

Thickets make good escape cover for almost every type of wild game. Brush breaks up the animal's outline and offers shade.

Tall grass makes excellent bedding cover. It provides a comfortable resting spot and offers animals camouflage from predators.

Moderately dense vegetation provides nesting cover for many upland birds. They prefer cover open enough so they can see and escape if necessary.

Glass for moose along forest edges, in willow swamps or near other feeding areas. Get to our vantage point early, so you can complete your stalk before the animals retreat to bedding areas.

Fertile croplands offer a good food supply. But expanses of corn and other row crops with little cover support few birds.

Look for early-season ringnecks scattered throughout crop fields, along grassy field edges and in brush patches.

In late season game concentrates in heavy cover like brush patches and farm groves.

Food and Water Needs

Hunters who understand the feeding habits and water needs of their quarry can better predict its daily movements. This makes it easier to select a good hunting location.

An elk may travel miles (km) to find food or quench its thirst, but most wildlife needs food and water in close proximity to cover. If an animal has to travel a long distance across open terrain to fulfill these basic needs, it is more visible to predators.

FOOD. Most game animals can adapt to a wide variety of foods. Researchers have found that bobwhite quail consume over 1,000 different foods including seeds, plants, nuts and insects.

Despite their ability to use such a wide range of foods, most animals select items that they can digest easily and that are high in proteins and calories. They seem to instinctively know which foods are most nutritious. In one study, squirrels gained weight when fed a diet consisting solely of white oak acorns. But they lost weight when fed acorns of red oak. In nature, squirrels commonly feed on acorns of white oak, but ignore those of red oak.

Like humans, game animals must have vitamins and minerals in their diet. Most animals obtain these vital elements from their food and water, but some need additional salt. They frequent springs and natural soil deposits with high salt contents. Many birds pick up grit not only to grind their food, but to provide needed minerals.

WATER. Birds generally require less water than mammals, because they can reuse water as it passes through their digestive tract. Gambel's quail can go a month or two without visiting a water hole. Pronghorns, on the other hand, need water each day.

Many game species can survive in areas with no lakes, streams or other sources of surface water. They obtain water from foods or dew.

A deer's diet varies throughout the year. Deer feed on twiggy browse, forbs (broad-leafed plants), grass, fruit, nuts, and moss. On scouting trips, identify and anticipate the food sources available during the season.

FOOD SOURCES

Natural foods are the mainstay in the diets of most game animals. A good supply of winter food is especially critical. Survival rates are generally low in years when winter food is scarce.

Food plots planted by wildlife agencies provide an additional source of food during winter, when natural food may be difficult to find. Some farmers leave a few rows of corn to sustain wildlife on their land.

Waste grain remains after farmers harvest their crops. It provides a temporary food supply for many animals like geese, ducks, pheasants and deer. They gather in large numbers to take advantage of this easy source of food. Waste grain may provide food throughout the winter where fields are left unplowed.

Common Types of Habitat

Some game animals can adapt to almost any kind of habitat. White-tailed deer, for instance, live in places as diverse as Florida swamps, southwestern deserts and river valleys of the Pacific Northwest. But most types of wildlife have more specific habitat requirements.

When hunting in unfamiliar territory, it pays to spend a good deal of time scouting. Conditions may not be right for spotting game, but you can always recognize good habitat.

Many types of wildlife have cover, food or water needs so specific that merely finding a broad habitat type is not enough. For example, moose prefer young conifer-hardwood forests. But within these forests, they seldom stray far from stream banks, lakeshores or willow bogs, their main feeding sites. Sage grouse live in semi-arid brushlands, but rarely venture more than 1.2 mile (1.93 km) from a water hole or other source of water.

As the seasons change, many species of game migrate to different types of habitat. In late fall, waterfowl leave northern marshes en masse. Most

winter in the South, resting and feeding on large lakes and in crop fields. As winter approaches, some types of mountain wildlife migrate to lower elevations, wintering in grasslands that offer more food and a less severe climate.

Hunting pressure may also force animals from their preferred habitat. Elk favor grassy mountain meadows, but when hunters begin to invade their territory, they retreat to higher, more rugged terrain where a person on foot could not follow. Waterfowl abandon many small lakes and ponds once the season opens. They seek refuge in the open water of large lakes and reservoirs.

In agricultural areas, wildlife may have to use other cover once crops are harvested. Pheasant hunters usually find the birds in crop fields during early season. But when the crops are removed, the birds move to permanent heavy cover like cattail swamps and woodlots.

Throughout this book, I identify the habitats most commonly associated with each species of game. Following are the major habitat types to which I refer.

WATER SOURCES

Surface water is a requirement for many species. Popular watering sites (left) include streams, lakes, human-made ponds and natural springs.

Succulent foods, like prickly pear cactus, provide water in arid climates. Rabbits and grouse often get water from grasses and buds.

Frost or dew also provides water in dry climates. To use this water source, animals must feed in early morning before the plants dry off.

Grasslands usually have grasses growing in combination with broad-leaved green plants or forbs. The height of the vegetation varies from less than 18 inches (46 cm) in arid habitats to 10 feet (3 m) where the soil is moist.

Coniferous forests have dense stands of needle- or scale-leaved evergreen trees that provide some cover. Needles that fall to the ground decompose slowly, forming acidic soil which produces few wildlife foods.

Brushlands have shrubs mixed with grasses and forbs; some have widely-spaced trees. The vegetation may be so thick that it is impenetrable. Brushlands are often an intermediate stage between grassland and forest.

Deciduous forests, also called hardwood forests, contain trees that lose their leaves in the fall. The leaves rot quickly, forming rich humus. Buds, nuts, shrubs and green plants provide food for wildlife.

Mixed forests have a blend of conifers and hardwoods. The combination of a good food supply and abundant cover enables these forests to produce more wildlife than coniferous or deciduous forests alone.

Wetlands have pockets of open water and dense stands of emergent vegetation like cattails and cane. The open water produces food for waterfowl and the fringes provide cover for a wide variety of game.

Semi-arid deserts contain shrubs, grasses and cactuses and may have some trees. They support more types of game than arid deserts, which have only scattered shrubs and cactuses.

Agricultural lands with a variety of cover types support a diversity of wildlife. The fertile soil produces abundant food and larger animals than most other types of habitat.

Chapter 2

HUNTING SKILLS
AND EQUIPMENT

When you choose the path of the hunter, you adopt a lifestyle and an outlook uniquely suited to the chase. It is a pursuit that quickens the heart and sharpens the focus. And the life skills and attitudes formed cross over into other facets of life. Hunting skills are gained over the course of several seasons and there is always more to learn, keeping you fit, vital and interested.

Gear to fit the small game hunter differs from that suited to the waterfowler. And the way of the traditional bowhunter is widely divergent from the style of the rifleman. Yet all share a bond and an ethos.

The complete hunter is versed in many skills and knows the operating systems and the nomenclature of a variety of tools. Most learn to hunt with a .22 rifle and then graduate to a centerfire rifle and shotgun. With knowledge of rifle and shotgun comes a passing acquaintance with ammunition and ballistics.

Some hunters opt to shoot a bow. The traditional bow (recurve or longbow) is a good place to start to learn the mechanics of archery. Next comes the compound bow, with its unique technical features and shooting style.

Hunters may opt to hunt with a muzzleloader rifle for a variety of reasons. It too comes with the need to gather knowledge and insight. There are several ignition systems, various powders and an array of projectiles designed to fit specific situations.

There is a lot to learn, but the process is rewarding. Along the way, the hunter faces challenges, but also finds satisfaction, building on successes in the field. Soon, success begins to show with meat on the table and trophies in the living room.

THE HUNTING RIFLE

A rifle that suits your style of hunting greatly increases your chances of success. When selecting a rifle, consider its action, weight and caliber.

ACTION. The action of a rifle refers to the design of the mechanism for chambering ammunition and ejecting spent cartridges. Single-shot actions, like the falling block, are extremely reliable because they have few moving parts. Their rigid mechanisms hold the cartridge firmly, resulting in a high degree of accuracy. These rifles must be reloaded after each round is fired, so they teach shooters to make the first shot count.

Repeating actions hold several cartridges in the magazine, making it possible to fire more than one shot without reloading. Like single shots, bolt actions have a rigid design and few moving parts. Many hunters consider the bolt action to be the most accurate and reliable rifle. Lever, pump and semi-automatic actions are designed for faster firing. You may need a quick second shot if you fail to kill the animal or if a branch deflects your bullet. But fast-action rifles have more moving parts, increasing the chance of mechanical failure, especially in cold weather or when dirt gets into the action.

WEIGHT. Rifles commonly weigh between 6 and 9 pounds (2.7 and 4 kg) without cartridges, slings or scopes. The recoil or kick, of a rifle depends mainly on its weight and its cartridge/caliber combination. Within a given combination, a heavy rifle has the least recoil, because the weight absorbs much of the energy that would otherwise be transmitted to your shoulder. Heavy rifles are easiest to hold steady and generally result in more accurate shots. Light rifles are easier to carry over a long distance.

The term carbine denotes a light rifle with a short barrel. Some hunters prefer carbines when hunting in heavy cover, where a longer rifle would tend to catch on brush or tree limbs.

CALIBER. The caliber of a rifle refers to the diameter of the barrel opening or bore. Caliber is measured in hundredths or thousandths of an inch or in millimeters. Hunters use rifles as small as .17 caliber for small animals and rifles up to .458 caliber for big game. Many rifle models are available in a choice of several calibers. Within a particular model of bolt action there may be fifteen different calibers.

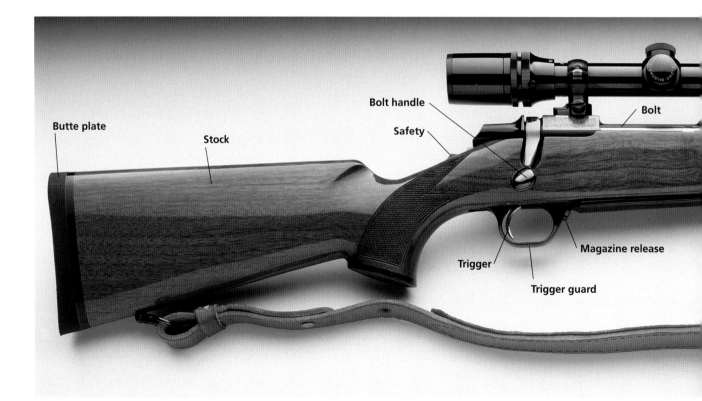

Popular actions include: (1) falling block and (2) lever actions, which chamber and eject cartridges by means of a lever under the trigger guard; (3) bolt action, in which the cartridge locks in place by moving the bolt forward and downward, much like a door bolt; (4) pump or slide action, which chambers and ejects by sliding the forearm back and forth; (5) semi-automatic or autoloader action which chambers and ejects cartridges automatically after each shot. The action is powered by gases from the burning powder or by the recoil.

Hunters are often confused by traditional caliber designations. A .30-06 rifle has a 0.3-inch-diameter (7.6 mm) bore. The 06 refers to 1906, the year the rifle was introduced. A .30-30 rifle also shoots a .30 caliber bullet. The bullet was originally propelled by 30 grains of smokeless powder. To further complicate the matter, some caliber designations do not refer to the diameter of the bore. For example, the bore of a .308 Winchester rifle does not measure 0.308 inch (7.8 mm). The .308 refers to the groove diameter or the diameter to the outside of the rifling grooves. The bore diameter is only 0.3 inch (7.6 mm).

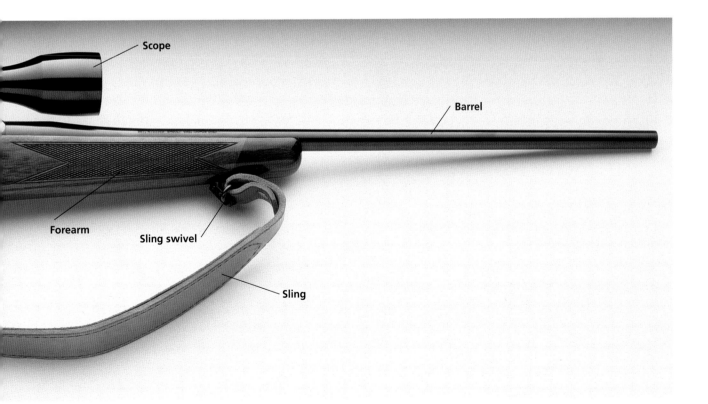

Scope

Barrel

Forearm

Sling swivel

Sling

RIFLE AMMUNITION

A hunter's choice of ammunition depends mainly on the size of the animal hunted and the distance at which it may be encountered.

To determine the ammunition best-suited for the game, consult a ballistics table. Most ammunition catalogs contain ballistic information including bullet energy, muzzle velocity and drop, all at different ranges.

A bullet's hitting power, or energy, is determined by its weight and velocity. The heavier and faster the bullet, the more energy it delivers to the target. At normal shooting ranges, a light, fast bullet generally delivers as much energy and kills as effectively as a heavier but slower bullet. Hitting power is measured in foot-pounds (Newton-meters).

Muzzle velocity or bullet speed is measured as distance traveled per second. The faster the bullet is, for a given weight, the more energy it carries. It also flies flatter. When comparing bullets of the same size, the more powder the case holds, the more velocity a bullet has. The size of the brass case affects how much powder is behind the bullet.

The bullet's performance is affected by its size, weight and shape. The bullet's size or diameter is referred to as its caliber. This diameter corresponds to the diameter of the rifling in the gun. Caliber is measured in decimal fractions of an inch, i.e., .300 or .30 is a 30 caliber. Some calibers are expressed in millimeters. So a 7 mm is approximately a .280; 6 mm is a .240; and 7.5 mm is approximately a .300.

Bullet weight is measured in grains.

The shape of a bullet determines its friction or resistance in the air, affecting its trajectory or flight path. A long, thin, streamlined pointed bullet retains its velocity at longer ranges better than a short, stout bullet. So the longer bullet has a flatter trajectory. Trajectory is also affected by the bullet's velocity. A fast bullet flies flatter than a slow one.

The construction of a bullet also determines its ability to penetrate upon impact. The bullet should mushroom on impact and not break apart. Mushrooming transfers all the bullet's energy into the target.

Certain ammunition shoot better in your rifle; each gun is a little different. Today's factory loads can perform up to the highest standards. Try different brands and loads until you find a particular cartridge that meets your needs and with which you can shoot tight groups.

Never use ammunition other than that recommended for the rifle by the manufacturer. The result could be a damaged rifle and serious injury. The correct cartridge designation for the rifle is stamped on the barrel next to the receiver or chamber.

Center-fire cartridges (far left and below) consist of: a brass case; a primer containing a highly explosive compound that ignites when struck by the firing pin; powder, which is ignited by the priming compound; a lead bullet, which may have a copper-zinc jacket to control the bullet's expansion. With rimfires (near left), the firing pin strikes the edge of the rim, igniting the priming compound.

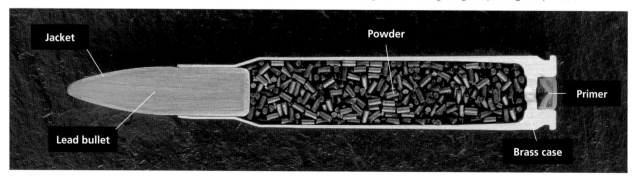

Jacket

Powder

Primer

Lead bullet

Brass case

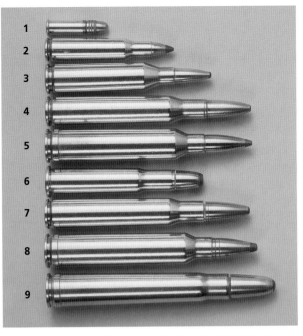

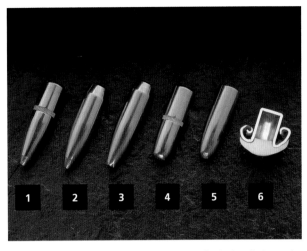

Bullet styles include (1) pointed, streamlined for high velocity and flat trajecto-ry. (2) Pointed boat tail has a tapered base to reduce drag even more. (3) Hollow points mushroom rapidly, but no faster than (4) flat and (5) round points, often used in rifles with tubular magazines. Their blunt points do not detonate cartridges ahead of them, but result in relatively slow flight and short range. (6) Mushroomed bullet shows expansion.

Cartridge types include: (1) .22 Long Rifle 40 Grain, (2) .222 Remington 50 Grain, (3) .243 Winchester 100 Grain, (4) .270 Winchester 130 Grain, (5) 7 mm Remington Magnum 150 Grain, (6) .30-30 Winchester 170 Grain, (7) .30-06 Springfield 150 Grain, (8) .300 Winchester Magnum 180 Grain, (9) .375 H&H Magnum 270 Grain.

TYPE OF CARTRIDGE (not actual size)	Muzzle Velocity (in fps)	ENERGY (in foot pounds)				TRAJECTORY				
		100 yds	200 yds	300 yds	400 yds	100 yds	150 yds	200 yds	300 yds	400 yds
.22 Long Rifle 40 Grain	1255	92	—	—	—	0.0	−11.5	—	—	—
.222 Remington 50 Grain	3140	752	500	321	202	+2.2	+1.9	0.0	−10.0	−32.3
.243 Winchester 100 Grain	2960	1615	1332	1089	882	+1.9	+1.6	0.0	−7.8	−22.6
.270 Winchester 130 Grain	3060	2225	1818	1472	1180	+1.8	+1.5	0.0	−7.4	−21.6
7 mm Remington Magnum 150 Grain	3110	2667	2196	1792	1448	+1.7	+1.5	0.0	−7.0	−20.5
.30-30 Winchester 170 Grain	2200	1355	989	720	535	+2.0	0.0	−4.8	−25.1	−63.6
.30-06 Springfield 150 Grain	2910	2281	1827	1445	1131	+2.1	+1.8	0.0	−8.5	−25.0
.300 Winchester Magnum 180 Grain	2960	3011	2578	2196	1859	+1.9	+1.6	0.0	−7.3	−20.9
.375 H&H Magnum 270 Grain	2690	3510	2812	2228	1747	+2.5	+2.1	0.0	−10.0	−29.4

Ballistics tables help determine the effective killing range of the cartridge and bullet drop at various ranges. This table lists muzzle velocity and the energy in foot-pounds delivered at ranges from 100 to 400 yards (91 to 364 m). As a rule, use a cartridge with at least 900 foot-pounds (1,220 N-m) to kill a deer, 1,500 (2,031) for an elk and 2,100 (2846) for a moose. Trajectory figures show how far the bullet strikes above (+) or below (-) the point of aim at ranges from 100 to 400 yards (91 to 364 m).

SIGHTS

The sighting system you use is as important as the rifle and ammunition. Some hunters spend as much for a rifle scope as they do for the rifle itself.

Many rifles come with iron sights. To aim, center a post at the end of the barrel in a notch or peephole in the rear sight. Iron sights are inexpensive, lightweight, durable and best-suited for short-range shooting.

For more accurate, precise shooting or for shots at longer distances, hunters prefer telescopic sights or scopes. A scope consists of a metal tube containing a system of lenses that magnify the target. The reticle, a network of lines or crosshairs inside the scope, enables you to aim precisely. The optics allow you to focus your eye on the reticle and target at the same time, so you can aim quickly. Scopes are not as durable as iron sights and are easier to knock out of adjustment.

Scopes vary in magnification power, from lx, which magnifies the target 1 time, to 12× or more. Fixed power scopes have one magnification power. Variable power scopes allow you to change the magnification with the twist of an adjustment ring. Most hunters use scopes ranging in power from 2× to 9×. Low-power scopes work best for close-range shooting. They have a larger field of view, making it easy to find your target. High-power scopes narrow the field of view, but help you see a distant animal.

A scope is attached to the gun using mounts or bases and rings. Whatever the mounting system, it must fit the scope, attach solidly to the gun and be adjusted to provide enough distance between the scope and your eye. Scopes should be at least 3 inches (7.6 cm) away from your eye, when the gun is shouldered, to allow for clearance when the gun recoils.

Most manufacturers offer a selection of special-purpose scopes designed specifically for shotguns and muzzleloaders.

Four-plex reticles have wires that are thick toward the outside. These wires stand out against the background and draw your eye to the target. The thin crosshairs enable you to aim precisely, without obscuring the animal.

Open sights have a blade or post, which must be centered in the notched rear sight. They are the most difficult of the sights to align and the rear sight covers up part of the target.

Peep sights require you to center the target in a hole in the rear sight, then place the bead directly on the animal. Hunters prefer large peep-holes so they can see most of the target.

Crosshair reticles work best for long-range shooting. The fine wires provide a precise aiming point and cover little of the target. But the wires may be difficult to see in dim light.

SIGHTING IN YOUR RIFLE

Every season, hunters miss their chance at a trophy because their rifles were not sighted in. Many people think that bore-sighting is sufficient. It is not. A bore-sighted rifle may shoot 20 inches (50.8 cm) or more from point of aim. Before hunting, take several practice sessions with your hunting ammunition.

You can sight in most easily at a shooting range. Most ranges have bench rests and sandbags to provide a steady rest and minimize human error. If sighting in your rifle in the field, make sure you shoot into a solid backstop.

To shoot accurately, take a deep breath, exhale halfway, then hold your breath as you squeeze the trigger. Do not jerk the trigger as you shoot.

Sights on a new rifle may be so far out of adjustment that you miss the target completely. To solve this problem, bore sight your rifle. Look directly through the bore of the bolt or falling block action. You cannot look directly through the bore of most other actions, so you must use a bore-sighting tool.

You can also rough-sight your rifle by simply aiming at a close target through the sights, firing, then making any adjustments needed to hit the bull's-eye.

Once you have rough-sighted at 25 yards (23 m), back off to 100 yards (91 m). Continue to fine-tune the sights until you can center the shot group on the bull's-eye. If you plan to shoot at longer ranges, sight in a few inches (cm) high at 100 yards. Then try a few long-range shots and make any necessary adjustments.

Always hunt with the same type of ammunition you used to sight in. Changing brands or bullet weights often makes it necessary to realign your sights.

Rest the forearm and butt stock on sandbags when sighting in. Do not support the barrel; the result will be inaccurate shooting. Hold the stock firmly against your shoulder. Always wear eye and ear protection when on the range.

Sight in your rifle so the bullet hits just above the point of aim at 100 yards (91 m). For most flat-shooting cartridges, you should zero-in 2 to 3 inches (5 to 7.6 cm) high; the exact distance depends on the trajectory of your bullet. By sighting in this way, you can aim dead-on at your target at any range up to 300 yards (274 m). The bullet hits slightly high or low, depending on the range, but strikes somewhere in the animal's vital area.

HOW TO ROUGH-SIGHT A RIFLE

Move the rifle barrel until the center of the bore lines up with the bull's-eye of a target 25 yards (23 m) away. Fix the rifle's position so it cannot move, then adjust the sights to aim at the bull's-eye.

Fire a three-shot group. The center of the group is the average point of impact. If the center is not in the bull's-eye, adjust the sights. With a scope you should strive to get a group size of 1 inch (2.5 cm) wide at 100 yards (91 m).

HOW TO ADJUST RIFLE SIGHTS

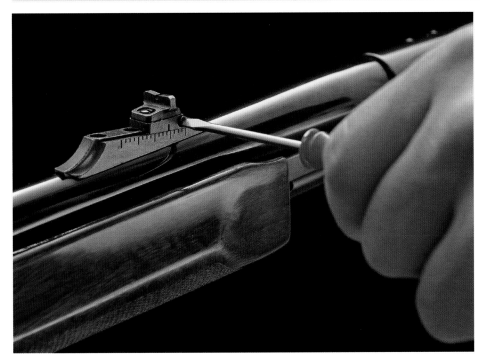

Adjust iron sights by moving the rear sight in the direction you want the rifle to shoot. To make the rifle shoot higher, raise the rear sight. To make it shoot to the left, move the rear sight to the left.

Move scope sights by turning elevation (up-down) and windage (right-left) screws the way you want the bullet impact to move. Read the instruction manual to see how much each click or mark changes the sight at 100 yards (91 m).

SHOOTING A RIFLE

Shooting a rifle under hunting conditions is more difficult than shooting at a target range. To shoot accurately, hunters must assume a stable position and know how to compensate for wind, uphill or downhill angles and moving animals.

Whenever possible, try to find a stable object to provide a steady rest for your rifle. If you cannot find such an object, the prone position is your next best choice. But shooting from the prone position may be impossible if ground cover or rolling terrain obscures your line of sight. Under these conditions, experienced hunters use the sitting position, which offers good stability because both elbows rest on the knees. The kneeling position is less stable, because only one elbow rests on the knee. The offhand position is the least stable. However, it may be the only choice when a moving animal offers a brief chance for a shot.

Learn how to adjust for natural forces like wind drift and the slant range effect. A strong crosswind dramatically affects a bullet's flight path. To hit a standing target, you must compensate by aiming slightly upwind.

The slant range effect causes your bullet to hit high whenever you shoot uphill or downhill. This confusing phenomenon results from the fact that gravity acts at a right angle to the horizontal. When a bullet is shot on a horizontal plane, gravity pulls at a right angle over the entire distance to the target, resulting in a curved flight path. But when a bullet is shot vertically, either straight up or straight down, gravity does not bend the flight path at all. The closer the angle to the vertical, the less the flight path curves.

A rifle is usually sighted in on the horizontal plane, so the sights are adjusted to compensate for maximum bullet drop. Since the bullet does not drop as much when shooting uphill or downhill, it always hits high. To compensate, aim low.

Most hunters tend to shoot behind running animals. A hunter using 150-grain .30-06 bullets would maintain a 4- to 5-foot (1.2 to 1.5 m) lead at a deer running at a right angle 100 yards (91 m) away. At 200 yards (183 m), he would increase the lead to about 10 feet (3 m) and at 300 yards (274 m), to about 16 feet (5 m).

Practice your lead by shooting at a rolling tire with a cardboard target wedged inside. Position yourself on a hill, then have someone roll the tire past you.

BULLET DRIFT

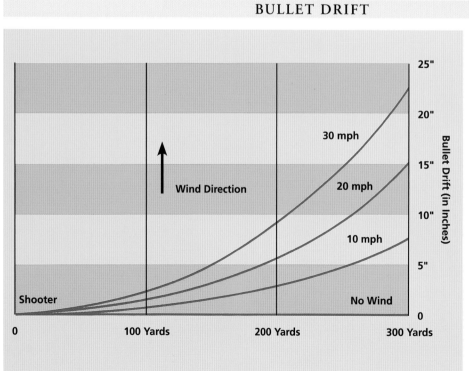

Wind drift increases as wind velocity and range increase. The chart shows how crosswinds of 10, 20 and 30 mph (16, 32, 48 km/h) would affect the path of a .30-06, 150 grain bullet at 100, 200 and 300 yards (91, 183, 274 m). As the chart indicates, a 10 mph crosswind would cause the bullet to drift less than 1 inch (2.5 cm) at 100 yards. But in a 30 mph crosswind, the bullet would drift over 22 inches (56 cm) at 300 yards.

Prone. Lie with your body about 30 degrees left of your line of aim. Place your left elbow just left of the rifle. Pull your right leg forward to lift your stomach off the ground, so your breathing does not affect the shot.

Kneeling. Sit on your right foot with your body 45 degrees left of the line of aim. Place your left foot forward and your left elbow on the knee.

Offhand. Stand sideways with feet perpendicular to the line of aim. Spread your legs to shoulder width. Keep your left elbow close to your body.

Solid rest. Rest your left hand or elbow on a solid object, like a tree or rock. Do not rest your rifle directly on the object.

Sitting. If you shoot right-handed, sit with your legs about 30 degrees to the right of your line of aim and rest your elbows firmly on your knees. Sitting is the most useful shooting position. You can use the position almost anywhere, assume it quickly and shoot accurately.

SHOTGUNS

Frontiersmen referred to the shotgun as a scattergun because it sprayed a swarm of lead pellets. A shot swarm is more effective than a single bullet for hitting moving targets.

When selecting a shotgun, consider the following: size of the bore, the chokes you need or the amount of barrel constriction, action, chamber length, weight and barrel type.

BORE SIZE. Shotgun bores are measured in gauge or in inches. As the gauge number increases, the size of the bore decreases. The most common gauges are 12 and 20, but gauges range from as small as 28 to as large as 10. The smallest bore is the .410, the only bore measured in inches. The larger the bore, the more pellets a gun can shoot. The denser shot pattern increases the chances for a long-range kill.

CHOKE. The amount of constriction or choke, at the end of the barrel affects the diameter and density of your shot pattern. Common chokes, from widest (most open) to narrowest (tightest), include: cylinder, skeet, improved-cylinder, modified, improved-modified and full. Open chokes are best for close-range shooting; tight chokes, long-range. The improved-cylinder is a good all-around choice.

Many modern shotguns have interchangeable screw-in choke tubes that enable you to quickly change chokes to suit the type of hunting. A gunsmith can also install screw-in chokes in some older guns.

Hinge action. The action opens when you push a lever or button at the rear of the receiver, allowing you to manually insert the shells. After firing, you break the action again. If your gun has ejectors, the spent hulls pop out automatically; otherwise, you must remove them yourself.

ACTION. Most single-shot and double-barreled shotguns have a hinge action. The simple hinge design is more reliable than repeating actions, like the pump and semi-automatic. Pump shotguns are more dependable than semi-automatics, which can malfunction in cold weather.

A pump gun ejects the spent shell and chambers another one each time you slide the fore-end back and forth. The majority hold five shells.

A semi-automatic fires one shell, ejects it and chambers another with each pull of the trigger. Most hold five shells, although a few hold up to seven.

CHAMBER LENGTH. Many shotguns are chambered for standard 2¾ shells. To shoot many types of magnum loads, you need a gun with a longer chamber. The proper shell length is usually engraved on the barrel. Never shoot a shell that exceeds that length.

WEIGHT. A light shotgun works best for quick shots in heavy cover. When you have more time to shoot, a heavier gun works better. You can hold the barrel steadier and swing on a target more smoothly.

BARREL TYPE. A long barrel provides a long sighting plane and can improve shooting accuracy. But contrary to popular belief, a longer barrel does not mean a noticeable increase in shooting range.

Many guns come with ventilated ribs. A rib makes it easier to sight down the barrel and cools it quickly, an advantage for rapid-fire shooting.

Field loads are adequate for close-range shooting at squirrels and rabbits and for small to medium-sized birds. Standard loads work better at longer ranges and for larger animals. Many hunters believe that magnum loads greatly increase their shooting range. But a magnum of the same length as a standard load may actually have a slightly lower velocity and a shorter range. The advantage of a magnum is a denser shot pattern.

Some magnum shells have longer cases that hold even more shot and powder. A 12-gauge, 3-inch (7.5 cm) magnum, for example, contains 1⅞ ounces (53 gm) of shot and 4 dr. equivalents of powder. Its effective range is about 10 yards (9 m) longer than a standard 2¾-inch (7 cm) load. Never attempt to shoot a long-cased magnum shell in a gun chambered for standard shells.

HOW CHOKE AFFECTS THE SHOT PATTERN

Choke determines how quickly your shot spreads. With a 12-gauge, improved cylinder choke and a standard-load No. 6 shell, about 13 pellets hit the vulnerable area of a stationary mallard silhouette at 40 yards (36.5 m). With a modified choke, about 16 pellets strike the target and with a full choke, about 20. Fewer pellets would strike a flying bird, because not all pellets in the shot swarm reach the target at the same time.

Proper fit should be checked while wearing your hunting clothes. You should be able to bring the gun to your shoulder in one motion, without the butt catching on your clothing. When you point the gun, the heel of your thumb should be 2 to 3 inches (5 to 7.6 cm) from your nose.

Screw-in chokes enable you to change your shot pattern for different types of hunting. These chokes screw into the barrel, so they have little effect on the gun's appearance. Use a specially designed wrench to install and remove the chokes.

RECOMMENDED SHOT SIZES

Game	Shot Sizes	Game	Shot Sizes
Cottontail Rabbit	6-7½	Turkey	4-6
Snowshoe Hare	4-6	Dove	6-8
Squirrel	5-7½	Woodcock	7½-9
Raccoon	6-7½	Small Duck	1-5
Ring-necked Pheasant	4-6	Medium Duck	1-4
Quail	7½-8	Large Duck	BB-3
Grouse	6-8	Medium Goose	BBB-1
		Large Goose	T-BB

Most often used for big-game hunting, slug loads are available in two basic styles: Sabot-type and Foster-style. While slugs are available for almost all gauges, 12-gauge slugs are the most popular.

Shooting a Shotgun

It takes little skill to hit a standing target with a shotgun, but moving game is a challenge. Expert shotgunners develop their skills through practice. You must adjust for different angles, ranges and flight speeds, all within seconds.

Because a moving animal offers only a brief shot opportunity, learn to mount the gun quickly and consistently. Place the butt against your shoulder and press your cheek against the stock. Keep both eyes open and sight down the barrel with your dominant eye, which for most right-handed shooters is the right eye.

Practice mounting the gun and operating the safety at home. Wear your hunting coat and make sure that you can bring the gun to your shoulder without it catching on your clothing. Quickly draw a bead on stationary objects. Rotate your shoulders and hips as if following a moving target. Be sure your shotgun is unloaded before you practice.

Shotgunners use three basic techniques for moving game. Snap-shooting works well at close range. But for crossing targets at longer distances, use the swing-through or sustained-lead method.

To sharpen your accuracy, shoot at practice targets or clay pigeons. Practice at a shooting range or have a friend throw clay pigeons with a hand trap. Fire at crossing, overhead and straight-away targets, so you learn how to shoot at different angles.

Most hunters tend to shoot behind crossing targets and below those that are rising, especially at long ranges. If you miss consistently, double your lead after each shot until you hit your mark.

THE SWING-THROUGH TECHNIQUE

Start your swing with the barrel behind the bird. Move the barrel smoothly and steadily, so it starts to catch up with the bird's tail.

Continue swinging so the barrel moves ahead of the bird. How far ahead depends on the distance and the speed and angle of the bird's flight.

Pull the trigger when you think you have reached the proper lead. Do not hesitate, flinch or slow down your swing as you pull the trigger.

Follow through until the barrel is well past the bird. If you stop swinging too soon, you will shoot behind the target.

BOWHUNTING

Taking a big game animal with a bow and arrow is one of hunting's biggest challenges. The hunter must practice many hours before the season begins; to learn to estimate range, draw the arrow smoothly, anchor it and place each shot in a target the size of a pie plate at 10, 20, 30, 40 and 50 yards (9, 18, 27, 36 and 46 m). And the bowhunter needs to refine his or her hunting skills as well as shooting skills.

Bowhunting is popular for many reasons: Hunters using a bow are generally allowed longer hunting seasons; this form of hunting is a big challenge; it is a relaxing and peaceful form of hunting. And it is fun!

There are basically three types of bows: the compound bow, the recurve bow and the longbow. Your choice of bow type is largely a matter of personal preference, each having its advantages and disadvantages.

The most popular hunting bow is the compound, which uses cams and cables to give the bow let-off, a reduction in the amount of force needed to hold the bow at full draw. This is an advantage when holding the bow back while waiting for a shot opportunity.

The peak draw weight, or maximum amount of weight needed to draw the bow, can be adjusted on a compound bow, whereas on a longbow or recurve, the draw weight is determined by the design of the bow. For a given draw weight a compound bow produces more energy than a recurve or longbow.

To determine draw weight, start by trying different bows. Select a bow with a draw weight that you can draw very comfortably. One of the biggest problems bowhunters have is trying to hunt with bows that have excessive draw weight.

Bows with a 60-pound (27 kg) draw weight are heavy enough for all North American game animals. In truth, it is the kinetic energy—not a bow's poundage—that matters most. Kinetic energy is a measurement based on the speed and weight of the arrow used. The higher the kinetic energy of an arrow, the more penetrating power or killing ability the arrow will have.

Kinetic energy is also affected by your draw length. This is the distance between the bowstring and the grip, when you hold a bow at full draw. Do not confuse draw length with arrow length; arrows are often shorter or longer than your draw length. For a given bow type, a

Consistent shooting practice includes knowing how the bow and arrow combination performs from different angles and at varied distances. Practice while wearing the clothing that will be worn on the hunt.

longer draw length produces more energy than a short draw length.

The design of the cams or wheels on compound bows also affects the bow's ability to produce energy. The more round the cam or cams are, the less arrow speed the bow is able to produce. However, they are easier to draw, more forgiving to shoot and are more quiet. Radical cams produce faster arrow speed, flatter trajectory and more energy, but they are also harder to shoot, more noisy and more difficult to maintain.

Arrow weight also affects the amount of energy that you can deliver into a target. A heavier arrow produces more energy. However, an arrow that is too heavy for a particular bow will not perform well. Consult an arrow selection chart or archery shop to help you choose the correct shaft.

Some hunters prefer to hunt with recurve and longbows. They are lighter, quieter to shoot and less prone to mechanical failure. These more traditional bows increase the challenge and add nostalgia to the hunt.

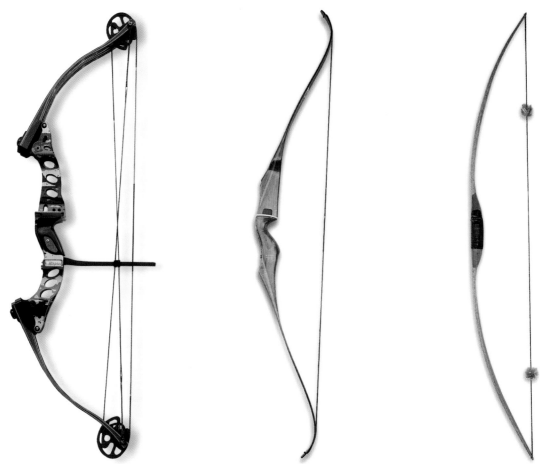

Bows include: (left) compound bows, (middle) recurve bows, (right) longbows. Compounds deliver the most energy for a given draw weight; longbows the least. A compound's limbs are made of manufactured materials. Recurves and longbows are usually made of fiberglass-wood laminates, though some longbows are solid wood.

Arrowheads include: (1) field points for practice, (2) steel blunts, (3) rubber blunts, (4) judo points for small game and field practice and (5) broadheads for hunting larger game.

Shooting a Bow and Arrow

In the hands of an experienced shooter, the bow and arrow can be very accurate. But the average hunter stands little chance of killing an animal with a bow, unless he or she is willing to take the time to practice.

Shooting a bow and arrow accurately is more difficult than shooting a firearm. You must build up the muscles you use to shoot, use the correct shooting mechanics and be able to concentrate. You also need to practice and develop your ability to judge distances accurately.

The first key to good shooting is the ability to relax. Learn to let the bow shoot the arrow. If you try to force the arrow into the target you will not shoot consistently.

A good stance is critical for accurate shooting. If your upper body moves around, your sights and bow will be moving, too. It is your legs that hold it all still.

Begin by standing with your feet spread apart at shoulder width, 90 degrees to the target. Then take a half-step back with the front foot and pivot slightly toward the target for a mildly open stance. Keep your weight evenly distributed on both feet and stand straight up, with your head directly over the center of your body. Maintain this stance as you raise the bow to shoot. Don't lean forward or backward to pull the bow and don't cock your head to the side to line up your sights. In some cases, you will not be able to shoot standing straight up, but try to position yourself in a way that gives you good upper body stability.

Your bow hand is placed on the handle slightly differently depending on the type of bow that you shoot. After selecting the correct grip for your bow type, remember that your hand should stay very relaxed as you draw the bow. You must be consistent with your hand position. Even slight variations affect the arrow flight.

Your string hand, like the bow hand, should stay relaxed throughout the drawing process. There are two basic styles that hunters use to hold and release bowstrings. The more traditional method is to use your fingers. If you release with your fingers, start by grasping the string at the first joints of your first three fingers, with the index finger above the nock, the other two fingers below the nock. As you draw, the middle finger should hold most of the weight and the other two fingers should float on the string. The other method for releasing the bow involves using a mechanical release aid. Choose one that has a rotating head, so it does not torque the string as you draw. With a wrist-strap release,

you should pull only on the strap and your fingers should remain loose. With a finger-held release, your wrist should stay straight and relaxed.

When you draw a bow, hold it at arm's length, roughly aiming at the target and begin to draw, pulling only with the muscles of your back. When you reach full draw, anchor solidly and aim at the target.

The anchor point for finger shooters is typically fairly high, with the tip of the index or middle finger planted solidly in the corner of the mouth. There is not necessarily a best way to anchor when using a release aid. With a wrist-strap release, many hunters anchor with the big knuckle of the index finger pressed behind the jaw. With a finger-held release aid, experienced shooters commonly anchor with the back of the hand pressed against the jaw.

No matter what type of equipment you use or the release method you use, the release should happen through complete relaxation. Focus your attention on pulling the bowstring with your back muscles. Release shooters pull the release trigger as their back muscles tighten up; finger shooters should let the string slip away as their hand relaxes. The shot should happen as a surprise.

Follow through a shot by holding your bow arm and release hand in the same position they were in when you released, until the arrow hits the target.

Always practice from the positions in which you hunt. If you use a tree stand, practice from an elevated platform. If you sit in your stand, practice in the sitting position. Wear your hunting clothes when practicing; they may affect your shooting. Use an arm guard to prevent the string from catching on heavy clothes.

Foot position and weight distribution are a critical part of a consistent shooting routine. Relax, spread feet to shoulder width, and orient the body toward the target in an open stance. The stance, the draw, and the release will become automatic with regular practice.

Low wrist position places the meaty party of the thumb on the bow handle. Maximum pressure falls about 1 inch (2.5 cm) below the big joint of the thumb. In this position, the wrist is more stable and less likely to move side to side.

Straight wrist grip is used with the recurve bow. At full draw, all pressure is between the thumb and forefinger.

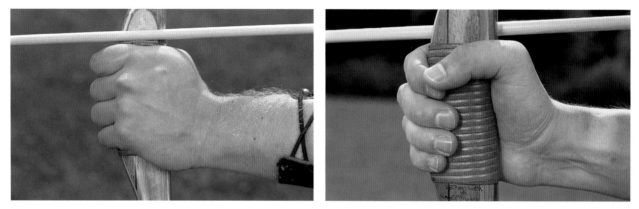

Low wrist grip (left) is standard form when shooting a longbow. Pressure should fall on the back edge of the heel of the hand (right). Gripping the bow with too much of the heel on the handle can cause the bow to twist during relapse, leading to poor arrow flight.

TYPICAL ANCHOR POINTS

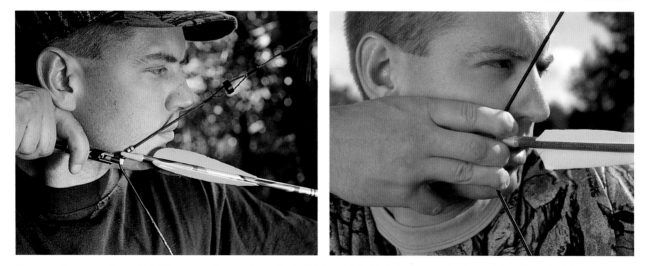

Using a wrist-strap release aid (left), many archers anchor with the big knuckle behind the jaw. With a finger-held release (right), most archers anchor so the tip of the index or middle finger is at the corner of the mouth.

Practice is critical to ensuring a clean kill. Skills honed on the range translate well to the woods.

BOW CARE TIPS

Inspect the bowstring before shooting; frayed strings should be replaced.

Oil axles every few days when in the field.

Keep your bow away from heat. Laminated bow limbs can come apart after only a few hours in a hot vehicle.

MUZZLELOADERS

Hunters who accept the challenge of making one shot count can hunt additional seasons when they start carrying a muzzleloader. Most states have special muzzleloader regulations that extend big-game hunting opportunities beyond normal gun seasons. Muzzleloaders or black powder guns must be loaded by inserting powder and bullet or shot into the muzzle, then pressing the load down the barrel toward the breech. Reloading after a shot can take a minute or more, requiring the first shot to be a good one.

Hunters have a choice between muzzleloading shotguns and rifles. Each one of these is available in different ignition systems. The three most popular include: in-line percussion caplock, percussion caplock and flintlock. Flintlock, the oldest ignition system, has never been very reliable for the hunter. The percussion caplock, developed in 1820, increased the muzzleloader's reliability. It wasn't until the mid-1980s that the first in-line muzzleloaders were developed. These frontloaders became a very reliable hunting weapon. The in-line design allows the percussion cap to be located very close to the powder charge, promoting quicker and more positive ignition.

The most popular muzzleloading rifles for big game are 50 or 54 caliber. The projectile may be a patched round ball or a conical or a saboted bullet. An in-line rifle firing a saboted bullet can achieve good accuracy at 100 yards (91 m), comparable to modern center-fires and have a killing range on whitetail-size animals out to 150 yards (137 m). The practical accuracy range of a patched round ball is approximately 80 yards (73 m); a conical, 100 yards. A modern in-line muzzleloader properly loaded with a heavy, well-constructed bullet is up to the task of downing any North American game animal.

A hunter today has a choice of types of powder to use in his gun. He or she can use the centuries-old black powder or a synthetic black powder called Pyrodex. Either type performs well and can be tested to see which one performs best.

Muzzleloading shotguns work well on waterfowl, upland game birds and turkeys. Small caliber muzzleloading rifles are used for small game and varmints. Be sure to check the regulations in the area you plan to hunt when using these muzzleloaders.

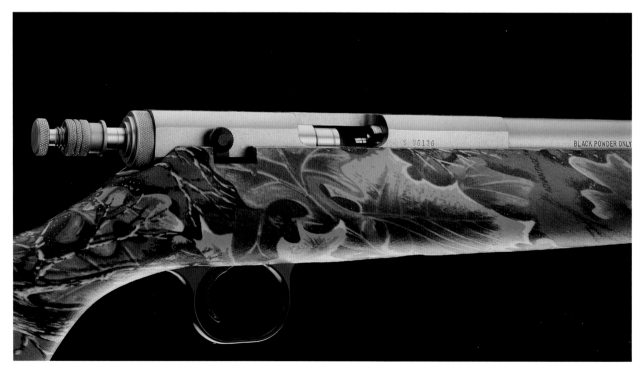

In-line percussion caplocks have an internal striker or hammer that is cocked by pulling it rearward. When the trigger is pulled, the striker slams forward and hits the percussion cap, which is positioned on a nipple. The nipple is positioned directly behind the powder charge, so the fire from the cap reaches it instantly.

OTHER COMMON IGNITION SYSTEMS

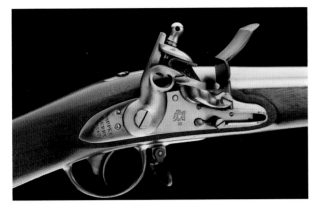

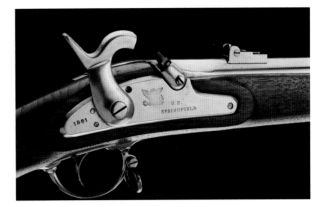

On a percussion caplock, the hammer strikes a percussion cap, similar to the primer of a modern cartridge. A flash travels through the nipple to ignite the powder charge.

Flintlocks have a flint in the hammer. When the flint strikes a frizzen, sparks ignite the primer powder. Flame passes through a vent hole to set off the powder charge.

PROJECTILES

Plastic sabots grip the bullet securely as they are pushed into the muzzle. At the same time, the lands of the rifling groove the sabot. When the gun is fired the sabot transfers the spin of the rifling to the bullet.

Conicals fit tightly into the barrel without the aid of patching materials. As a conical is pushed down the barrel, the lands of the rifling engrave the soft lead, forming a tight seal.

Patched round balls must fit correctly in the barrel to achieve accuracy. The ball never touches the inside of the barrel. The patch grips both the soft lead ball and the grooves of the rifling.

BULLET TRAJECTORY

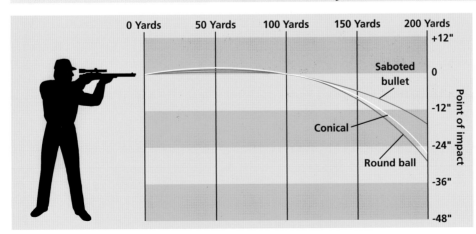

Bullet trajectory for saboted bullets is flatter than that of conicals and round balls. As the illustration shows, a saboted bullet sighted in at 100 yards (91 m) hits only 1½ inches (3.8 cm) high at 50 yards (46 m) and 6 inches (15 cm) low at 150 yards (137 m).

HUNTING SAFETY

Most people would be surprised to learn that hunting is not among the most dangerous sports. A National Safety Council study showed the fatality rate for hunting to be less than half that of boating or swimming.

Improved hunter education and increased use of fluorescent orange clothing account for the low accident rate. Every state and province sponsors some type of firearms safety or hunter education program. Many states require beginning hunters to pass such courses before they can purchase a license.

Nevertheless, the potential for a serious accident always exists. To avoid an accident, follow these safety rules.

- Treat every firearm as if it is loaded. Never assume a gun is unloaded because someone said so.
- Never point a weapon at anything you do not mean to shoot. This includes glassing other hunters with your rifle scope.
- Make sure your safety is on at all times, unless you intend to shoot.
- Positively identify your target before shooting. Never fire at a silhouette, a vague form or an area where you saw or heard something move. Fluorescent orange clothing greatly improves your own visibility.
- Control the direction of your muzzle at all times. If you start to fall, point the barrel away from yourself and other hunters. After a fall, check the barrel for obstructions like dirt or snow. A plugged barrel could rupture when you shoot, possibly causing serious injury.
- Never lean a gun against a tree, fencepost, vehicle or any place where it could fall over and accidentally discharge.
- Never shoot at hard surfaces or water with bullets or slugs. They could ricochet and strike another hunter or a building.
- Never drink alcoholic beverages before or during a hunt. Alcohol does not keep you warm; instead, it speeds the loss of body heat.
- Use only the ammunition recommended for your firearm. Do not carry two different types of ammunition in your pocket at the same time.
- When not hunting, keep the gun unloaded and the action open.
- Keep all firearms and ammunition out of the reach of children.
- Refuse to hunt with anyone who does not observe the basic rules of firearms safety.

Keep the safety on and your finger away from the trigger until you are ready to shoot. This eliminates the possibility of discharging the gun accidentally, especially if you stumble or fall.

PLANNING FIRING ZONES

Establish safe firing zones when hunting with others. When driving game, hunters should shoot only within their zone area.

Position your boat sideways to the shooting area. Do not position the boat lengthwise; this places one hunter in the other's shooting zone.

Split the area around your blind into 180-degree shooting zones. Each hunter scans for birds in the semicircle area around his or her half of the blind.

Never shoot unless you can see your target clearly. In dim light you may see a form that resembles a game animal (left). The right photo reveals that the form is actually that of a hunter.

OTHER SAFETY TIPS

Open your action before crossing a creek (left), climbing over a fence or in any other situation where you are unsure of your footing.

Never shoot if there is a chance of hitting buildings, livestock or any other unintended target. Avoid shooting over the tops of hills and ridges.

Carry your firearm so the muzzle points away from others. Safe positions include: shoulder carry, cradle carry and trail carry.

Chapter 3

HUNTING STRATEGIES

Whether you travel to another state or hunt the back forty, advance planning is the key to a good hunting trip. Lay the groundwork for your trip early.

Preparations for an out-of-state hunt should begin at least a year ahead. Some states conduct drawings for non-resident permits to hunt animals like elk, deer, pronghorn or moose. Most states accept applications until spring, but some set deadlines as early as mid-winter.

If you do plenty of scouting, it will pay off by helping you choose the right hunting method for the game and the area you hunt.

Begin planning your trip by requesting non-resident hunting information from the wildlife agency in the state or province where you plan to hunt. Be sure to specify the type of game you will be hunting. Ask about drawing application deadlines and information on state and federal wildlife areas that may require advance reservations. Licenses may be offered on a first-come, first-served basis. Some states require hunters to show evidence of having passed a firearms safety or hunter education course.

Reservations and permits may also be necessary when hunting in your own state. Wildlife managers and conservation officers can provide information on special hunts that require advance preparation. They can also supply current game census data to help you choose a hunting area. Managers may know of local farmers or ranchers who want hunters to thin over-abundant game populations.

Sportsmen's clubs like the Safari Club International, Rocky Mountain Elk Foundation, Mule Deer Foundation, and state hunting organizations are great places where hunters can network and share information. Some clubs lease private land where members can hunt.

SCOUTING FOR GAME

Pre-season scouting improves your odds of finding game once the hunting season begins. Best of all, scouting is enjoyable and saves valuable hunting time.

Scouting enables you to become familiar with the terrain and to identify heavily used game trails. It also helps determine any changes in habitat conditions or fluctuations in game populations that could affect the hunting.

Severe winter storms, wildlife food shortages, drought and cold or wet weather during nesting can drastically reduce game populations. New roads, housing developments and wetland drainage can permanently eliminate good wildlife habitat. So, there is no guarantee that last year's prime hunting spot will produce game this year.

Binoculars and spotting scopes help to locate game from a distant vantage point. But even if you do not see animals, you can detect their presence by the signs they leave. For instance, squirrels build nests in trees and scatter nut shells on the ground. Waterfowl preen themselves and leave feathers around resting areas. Bull elk bugle and roll in wallows during the mating period. All animals can be identified from their tracks and droppings. Damaged trees and brush result from animals rubbing velvet from their antlers, scratching trees to mark their territory or chewing bark.

Glass a potential hunting area from a nearby hill or tree. Look closely at edges between openings and cover to detect movement. You are most likely to see game early in the morning, at dusk or on cloudy days. When you spot an animal, note the time and identify a landmark to pinpoint the exact location. If the animal is not disturbed, it may appear in the same area at about the same time on subsequent days.

PLANNING TIPS

Always ask for permission to hunt on private land. Introduce yourself and specify the type of game you wish to hunt. Some landowners grant permission to a courteous hunter, even though their land is posted.

Talk to a clerk at a sporting goods store for local hunting information. Most carry maps, permit applications and other items for planning your hunt and many employ knowledgeable hunters.

Gather information from state and federal wildlife agencies. They supply maps, brochures on public hunting areas, public access lists and regulations. Tourist bureaus can recommend motels, resorts and campgrounds.

County maps identify paved and unpaved roads. They also show section lines, buildings, public lands, lakes and streams. Plat books detail property lines and identify landowners. The maps and plat books are usually available at county offices.

Aerial photographs reveal important details lacking on maps. They show isolated ponds and marshes, small streams, vegetation types, logging areas, meadows and forest trails. They can be obtained from the U.S. Department of Agriculture and private survey firms.

Topographic maps, like the U.S. Forest Service map and the U.S. Geological Survey map, provide information on land elevation and detail other features of the landscape, such as wetlands. They also show buildings, roads, trails, portages and other features useful for finding your way on a hunting trip. Geological Survey maps show forested areas in green. They generally cover a larger area than Forest Service maps.

Tracks in damp soil may reveal how long ago an animal passed. Fresh tracks (left) have sharp edges. Older tracks (right) have fuzzy edges. In snow, old tracks have a hard crust.

Droppings help hunters find game. Large quantities indicate feeding, loafing or bedding areas. Some animals do not digest their food completely, so you can check droppings to determine what they have been eating.

Feeding signs include damaged crops; scratched earth; nipped ends on grasses or twigs; and pits, husks and shells of fruits or nuts. Experienced hunters can often identify an animal by these signs.

Damaged trees and brush result fom animals rubbing velvet from their antlers, scratching trees to mark their territory, or chewing bark. Each species has distinctive rubs, scrapes and chews.

Beds and roosts in tall grass or on soft earth reveal the resting spots of mammals and birds. You can identify the animal from the size of its bed or roost and from nearby droppings, hair or feathers.

Game trails lead from cover to food or water. Several kinds of game often use the same trail. Inspect it closely and look for fresh tracks made by the animals you are hunting.

STILL-HUNTING

More people blow it while they're still-hunting than with any other method. The problem is that we move too fast. It's called still-hunting because most of the time the hunter should remain still, processing every sound, every movement, every smell.

Take a step, look and listen. Wait 30 seconds, 60 seconds or 5 minutes before taking the next step. Don't make a sound. Remember, you're in country you scouted. You know the game is close by. The success of the hunt hinges on the confidence you've placed in this piece of real estate.

Hunt into the wind. If the air movement shifts direction, change with it, keeping the breeze in your face. Move too fast and deer see you before you spot them. Slow down. Slow way down. Every time you take a step, a new window opens in the habitat. Look for the horizontal line of a back, the black of a nose, the flick of a tail, the crook of a leg or sunlight glinting from a nut-brown antler. Carry binoculars on a harness around the shoulders, not on the belt or in a daypack. And use them more than your boots.

In heavy cover, crouch down to look beneath the bushes. Sometimes that affords a better view through the stalks and the trunks. Maybe you'll spot a deer standing, listening to make sense of the sound you made when last you took a step. Sometimes you'll spot a deer looking back.

Place each footstep carefully to prevent snapping twigs, crunching leaves or brushing against branches. Avoid crossing open areas and places where animals could see your form above the horizon. Try to stay near cover where game will not notice your movements.

Still-hunting is usually a one-hunter method, but it also works well with two patient hunters. Game surprised by one person may run toward the other. Or an animal may be so intent on watching one human that it does not detect another approaching.

Successful still-hunting demands patience and confidence. If you lose patience and begin moving too fast, animals will spook. If you are confident of seeing game, it is easier to stay focused.

TIPS FOR STILL-HUNTING

Walk slowly and quietly (top). Avoid turning your head quickly, swinging your arms or making other movements that animals associate with humans.

Detect wind direction and rising and falling thermals (bottom) by squeezing unscented powder into the air or by tossing a small amount of down into the air.

Wear soft clothing to reduce noise. Hard-finish materials like nylon make swishing sounds as they brush the cover. Gummy boot soles enable you to walk quietly.

Look for visual clues to find game. A horizontal line among trees could be an animal's back. A glinting eye or twitching ear could also reveal game.

Avoid walking or waiting in direct sunlight. Animals are quick to notice the glare off your face and clothing. They are less likely to see a hunter in the shade.

STAND-HUNTING

To hunt from a stand, you must be positioned where you are likely to see game, but the game is not likely to see you. Concealment, awareness and confidence are the keys to success.

Hunters conceal themselves on stands or in blinds. A stand may be nothing more than a large tree that obscures your form. Or it may be an elevated platform, either free-standing or attached to a tree trunk or limb. A blind provides more cover. Many have walls of camouflage material or vegetation.

Whether hunting from a blind or stand, choose a spot where game is likely to pass. Take a scouting trip before the season to find first the water, then the feed, then the bedding ground. A deer will not make its living more than ½ mile (0.8 km) from its water source. Scout the area to find heavily-used game trails or escape routes. Take position well before game begins moving. You may have to find your spot in the dark.

Place a stand to take advantage of the view into well-used trails that lead from bedding areas to feeding areas. Or set up on the approach from bedding cover to water.

Take care to position the stand downwind from the trail and if the wind changes direction, find a different place to hunt until conditions improve. Select alternative locations for different wind conditions. To ensure that animals do not detect human scent, many hunters use odor eliminating products or masking scents.

Wind direction is also important when hunting ducks or geese on water. Choose a blind on the lee side of natural cover. Waterfowl usually land into the wind in the calmer water.

Stand-hunters sometimes wear camouflage outfits to reduce their visibility. But many types of hunting require high-visibility clothing for safety purposes. Even if you wear fluorescent orange clothing, game is less likely to see you if you keep motion to a minimum. If you must move, do so very slowly. Keep your face hidden; look at game from the side of your eye or from behind a hat brim.

Comfort is important when stand-hunting. You cannot remain quiet and motionless if you are cold, wet or in an uncomfortable position. You need warm clothing, because you must remain stationary for long periods. Some hunters build roofs to shed rain or use padded seats and stoves. Waterfowl hunters sometimes build blinds that are completely enclosed except for shooting windows.

Stand-hunting works best early or late in the day, when animals move between resting and feeding areas.

HOW TO SELECT A STAND-HUNTING LOCATION

Portable stands enable you to change location quickly. Some types clamp to the trunk in seconds. They have a comfortable seat and, when placed well above ground level, offer a wide field of vision. An elevated stand keeps your scent above the ground and places you higher than the usual sight plane of the game.

Locate your stand or blind near a watering site or stream crossing. Dove and antelope hunters often hunt near water holes. Moose hunters carefully check stream banks for heavily used trails leading to water.

Choose a site near a feeding area. Goose hunters build blinds or dig pits in harvest fields. Deer hunters take stands along the edges of corn, hay or milo fields. Bear hunters sometimes bait an area, then hunt nearby.

Select a stand site in a location where you are not silhouetted against the skyline. Game will detect your movement more easily if you do not have a backdrop.

Avoid stands that do not offer a clear field of fire. A tree or branch too close to your stand will narrow your shooting zone. A stand that restricts hip movement makes it difficult to swing your gun.

STALKING

To stalk an animal, you must see it first. Binoculars or spotting scopes help hunters to locate the quarry from far away and plan a strategy. A spotter who remains in a fixed location can signal to the stalker and direct the hunt from afar.

Like still-hunting, stalking demands fine-tuned hunting skills, because you must close the distance on game without being detected. Sneaking within shooting range can be extremely difficult, but expert stalkers may be able to approach within a few feet (m) of game.

When you spot an animal, watch it to determine whether it is likely to remain in the same area long enough for a stalk. If the animal is moving or appears nervous, you will probably not be able to get close enough for a shot. The odds are much better when the animal is feeding or is bedded.

Stalking works best where the topography or cover conceals the approach. Before beginning the stalk,

plot a course that takes you into the wind, but keeps you behind hills, trees, fence lines or other natural or man-made features.

If there is no cover, use a clump of vegetation to break up your outline. Camouflage clothing makes you less visible. Move only when the animal faces away from you or when its head is down. Be sure that sunlight does not reflect off your gun, scope or wristwatch.

Move silently during the final stages of the stalk. Noise may not be important if you shoot from 300 yards (274 m). But for the bowhunter who must approach within 30 yards (27 m), the slightest noise can ruin his or her chances.

It is usually best to stay concealed until after the shot. But waterfowl hunters sometimes rush the birds before they shoot. They may gain an extra 5 to 10 yards (4.5 to 9 m) before the birds take off.

Plan your stalk so you move directly into or quarter into the wind. This prevents the wind from carrying your scent and the sound of your approach to the animal.

Pinpoint game by identifying nearby landmarks like a tree, boulder or fencepost. You can stay hidden while using the landmark to guide your approach.

Use natural cover to conceal your approach. A fenceline, a drainage ditch or a field of tall crops of grass enables you to sneak within gun range.

Bring your own cover when hunting in flat, open country. Push a clump of weeds ahead of you and stay low so game cannot spot your form above the horizon.

DRIVING

A lone hunter has little chance of rousting game from a large expanse of cover. Most animals sit tight or move off to the side rather than run or fly.

Before the drive begins, posters sneak to positions at the end of cover, where they intercept game pushed to them by drivers. The drivers spread out across the field or woods. The denser the vegetation, the closer they must be to discourage game from doubling back between them. It is generally better to have more drivers than posters.

Drives work best in a corridor or block of cover surrounded by open land. Game usually stays in the cover until pushed to the end, assuring someone of a shot. If possible, start at the widest end and work toward the narrowest. This concentrates the animals in a relatively small area, increasing your chances of a close shot.

Hunters should always know the position of other drivers and posters. Wear fluorescent orange clothing for maximum visibility and never shoot in the direction of another hunter.

Driving is an effective way to push game out of cover. You can make a drive with as few as two or more than a dozen hunters, depending on the situation.

TIPS FOR DRIVING

Drivers should stay within sight of each other. Outside drivers often move ahead to prevent game from escaping out the sides. Be especially alert as drivers approach posters; cornered game may spring from cover.

Islands of cover are ideal for drives. A patch of high brush in an open field, a shelterbelt or a woodlot is likely to hold game. If you attempt to hunt these areas alone, game may escape out the opposite side.

Corridors of cover, like roadside ditches, canyons, stream courses and railroad tracks, make good places for a drive. Game is less likely to double back in a narrow strip of cover than in a wide expanse.

FLUSHING

For many types of game, the surest way to evade hunters is to hide in dense cover. Even animals as large as a deer or as brightly colored as a rooster pheasant can hide within a few feet (m) of hunters without being noticed.

Hunters who use dogs stand the best chance of flushing tight-holding animals. Even in thick brush or other dense cover, a good dog detects and follows an animal's scent. Without a dog, you are sure to walk by some game.

A lone hunter can unnerve animals, causing them to flush. Unusual sounds and erratic movements may cause game to become nervous and burst from cover. Many hunters yell, clap their hands, crack brush or even run a few steps to convince an animal that it has been discovered.

When hunting with a partner, try to flush game toward each other. Start at opposite ends of the cover in an attempt to trap game in the middle. This cuts off possible escape routes. And because the animal detects danger from two directions, it is more likely to flush.

Stop frequently when attempting to flush game. If you walk at a steady pace, animals usually sit tight because they are confident they have not been detected. When you stop, they lose confidence and attempt to escape.

TIPS FOR FLUSHING GAME

Throw sticks or rocks to flush game from dense brush piles or other cover too thick to walk through. Game usually attempts to slip out the opposite side, so watch carefully and be ready for a shot.

Kick or step on clumps of vegetation that could hold birds or small game. With a hunter this close, game may be reluctant to flush. Tracks, droppings, feathers or hair may reveal the animal's presence.

HUNTING DOGS

One of the hunter's most valuable assets is a well-trained hunting dog. Watching a good dog in action adds to the thrill of the hunt. And a dog with flushing, pointing or retrieving skills greatly improves your hunting success.

Before selecting a dog, consider the type of game you intend to hunt, the terrain and climate. Pointing and flushing breeds were originally developed for hunting upland birds, most retrievers for waterfowl and most hounds for small game. Many breeds work well for more than one type of game. The Labrador, for example, is an excellent waterfowl retriever, but is also favored by many upland bird hunters for its flushing skills.

When hunting upland birds in a large expanse of light cover, use a dog that ranges widely. Pointing breeds work beyond gun range. When they detect a strong scent, they freeze in position or point. This gives the hunter time to walk in and flush the bird. For finding birds in thicker cover, a flushing dog may work better. These dogs work the cover slowly and thoroughly, usually staying within gun range.

Thorny cover can penetrate the fur and cut a short-haired dog. Long-haired breeds can tolerate thorns, but their fur often becomes matted with burrs.

In cold weather, a heavy-coated breed retains body heat longer than a dog with a thin coat. A thick coat is especially important for a dog that must retrieve in icy water. In extremely hot weather, a thin-coated breed works best. A dog with thick fur would overheat quickly.

Learn to read your dog, because every dog behaves somewhat differently when it smells game. With a pointing dog, a loose point usually means that the game has slipped away. A staunch point generally means game is close. Retrieving and flushing breeds perk up their ears or wag their tails rapidly. Hounds bay when they detect game.

Proper training and conditioning are the keys to developing a good dog. A poorly trained dog is worse than no dog at all. If it does not obey basic commands, it may flush game out of range. Or the dog may run off, costing you hours of hunting time.

Pre-season conditioning helps a dog maintain its stamina and toughens its feet. Run your dog at least one-half hour several times a week during summer.

POPULAR HUNTING DOG BREEDS

Retrievers include the Labrador retriever, golden retriever, Chesapeake Bay retriever and American water spaniel. These breeds are well-suited for retrieving waterfowl, because their skin secretes an oily substance that sheds water. Most retrievers also flush and retrieve upland game birds.

Pointing breeds include the English pointer, German shorthair, Brittany spaniel, English setter, Gordon setter and weimaraner. These breeds are used for upland birds, but a few hunters use them for rabbits and squirrels. Many pointers also retrieve downed game.

Flushers include several types of spaniels, like the springer, cocker and Boykin. These breeds pursue game until it flushes from cover, so they should be trained to work within gun range. The springer is especially popular among pheasant hunters.

Hounds, like the black-and-tan and redtick, have highly sensitive noses and are used mainly for trailing small game. Some, like the beagle, also work well for game birds. Other hounds include the bluetick, Walker and redbone.

FLOAT-HUNTING

Float-hunting works best for waterfowl, squirrels, deer, moose and other animals that frequent stream banks and lakeshores. You can also float up on flocks or rafts of waterfowl in open water.

Most float-hunters use small, low-profile watercraft including jon boats, canoes, semi-Vs and sculling boats. Boats are usually painted camouflage colors or draped with natural vegetation, netting or camouflage cloth.

The best boat depends on the area you hunt and the type of hunting. A jon boat is very stable, but the square bow would not slide through dense cattails. A canoe or double-pointed duck boat is less stable, but would slip through easily. A deep semi-V is best for rough water, but because of its high profile would not be a good choice for floating up on waterfowl. The birds would be less likely to notice a shallow-draft, sculling boat.

Silence is the key to float-hunting success. You can paddle very quietly in a canoe. If you row a boat, make sure the oars do not squeak or scrape the gunwales. Keep loose items tied down and try not to move around

in the boat. Wood and fiberglass hulls are quieter than aluminum hulls. Many hunters glue carpet or rubber matting to the bottom, seats and gunwales to muffle sounds.

Keep safety in mind when float-hunting. Wear a life preserver. Never hunt from a tippy boat. It may flip over if you stand up to shoot or when your dog plunges into the water to retrieve game. To stabilize a canoe or other small watercraft, add pontoons or bands of buoyant material to the side of the hull. Low-profile boats make you less visible, but they can be dangerous on large, wind-swept waters.

To float-hunt a stream, float from one point to the next. The points conceal your approach, enabling you to slip up on game downstream.

You can pole through heavy cover, such as cane, cattails, bulrushes or other high vegetation to jump waterfowl and other game. Some hunters use push-poles as long as 16 feet (5 m) to propel narrow watercraft through the weeds. Or, you can use a duck-bill on your push-pole.

Water offers hunters an excellent means for a silent approach. A float-hunter can cover a large area with relatively little effort.

HOW TO FIND DOWNED GAME

Losing a wounded animal is one of the greatest frustrations in hunting. Finding downed game requires patience and persistence. But conscientious hunters make every effort to recover game that has been hit.

After the shot, watch the animal closely and try to determine if you made a clean kill, wounded it or missed completely. Clean kills and misses are usually obvious, but it may be more difficult to recognize a wounded animal. Even if you see no sign of a hit, look for hair or feathers, erratic movement or unusual behavior. You might hear the impact when your bullet strikes a big game animal.

Dogs with good retrieving skills greatly improve your chances of finding downed birds and small game. A dog marks a bird down and promptly retrieves it. If it runs, the dog circles to pick up the scent, then follows the scent trail.

Follow up any shot at big game, because large animals may show little evidence of being hit. Despite its size, a wounded deer can be as difficult to find as a cottontail. Unless hit in a vital area, it may run a long distance, especially if pursued by hunters.

If you are sure you hit a vital area, begin your pursuit immediately. An animal shot in the heart-lung area seldom runs farther than 100 yards (91 m). If you suspect a less damaging hit, it may be better to wait before following. A bleeding animal may lie down if not pursued. After 30 to 60 minutes, it will probably be too weak to run. Do not wait to follow if rain or snow threatens to obscure the blood trail.

Blood trails may provide clues for pursuing wounded game. Bright red, frothy blood indicates a lung shot and tells you to follow immediately. Darker blood usually means a less damaging hit; wait before following.

Mark the spot where you last saw the animal. Look for an obvious landmark, like a tree or leave a piece of clothing at the spot. Work outward in widening circles, but return if you fail to find the animal.

Look for feathers, hair or blood where you suspect the animal to be. Stand still, listen for movement, then inspect nearby cover. Hunters may fail to find game by leaving too soon, thinking the animal has run off.

Move quietly and watch ahead for movement when trailing big game. If you fail to see the animal and approach too closely, you may frighten it off, making it more difficult to find. Locating downed game is easiest with two or more hunters. While one inspects the ground for blood, the other looks for any signs of movement. If you lose the trail, mark the spot where you last saw blood. Then you can resume the search at that point.

Check likely escape routes if you cannot find the animal. Wounded game may slip into a strip of grass connected to the main cover area.

Examine thick clumps of grass or brush patches for signs of the animal. A protruding tail reveals the location of this wounded pheasant.

Work your dog just downwind of downed game. If the dog does not pick up the scent, call it to the spot where you last saw the animal.

Chapter 4

HUNTING BIG GAME

The concept of giving game "a sporting chance" is almost as old as hunting itself. It springs from the ethic of a skilled hunter who appreciates the challenge of the hunt as much as the meat or the trophy.

There is no sport with a richer tradition and no sport as demanding or rewarding as the hunt for big game. To be successful, the hunter has to develop an understanding of the quarry.

An animal's daily movements may be predictable or unpredictable, based on the species, the terrain, the weather and available feed. Scouting helps the hunter learn which trails animals are using between bedding areas and feeding areas. Such information allows the hunter to make an educated decision about where to still hunt, spot and stalk or set a tree stand.

Big game hunters should know how to use a map, a compass and survival gear. It is easy to become disoriented in the mountains, in the plains or in the fog. Study aerial photos or topographic maps before hunting and carry maps while hunting. Identify prominent landmarks in the field. Study of maps and photos will also open up new potential hunting spots.

Proper physical conditioning can make hunting more enjoyable, especially in steep or mountainous terrain. If you are out of condition or have blisters on your feet, it can be a chore to walk up a hill with a rifle and backpack, let alone drag out a large animal.

There is no sport more challenging, demanding or rewarding than the hunt for big game. The individual must match wits with an animal perfectly suited to its habitat. And the reward is great: a sense of accomplishment, perhaps a trophy and a supply of prime, high-quality meat.

WHITE-TAILED DEER

More people hunt for whitetail than for any other big game animal in North America. For many hunters, taking a trophy whitetail buck is the ultimate challenge.

The typical whitetail doe or buck is a high-strung, elusive creature that is very aware of its surroundings, whether it is at rest, feeding or on the move.

In a Michigan experiment, 39 deer including 7 bucks, 14 does and 18 fawns were fenced inside a 1-square-mile (2.6 sq km) area. Six experienced hunters attempted to find one deer. On the fourth day, one hunter finally spotted a buck. After one month, the average amount of time needed for a hunter to spot a buck was 51 hours. It took an average of 14 hours to spot any deer.

The deer's home range is small, so its very survival is based on its keen senses, its ability to find concealment and its intimate knowledge of its home range.

Whitetails rely on their sense of smell to detect danger. They can catch a whiff of human scent from hundreds of yards (m) away. Deer also hear extremely well. They do not have particularly sharp eyesight, but they are quick to detect lateral movement. Deer are not color-blind. Researchers have discovered that deer can perceive some color.

Whitetails often elude hunters by sitting tight in grassy or brushy cover. Their coats blend in perfectly. A hunter may pass within a few feet (meters) of a deer and not see it.

Deer are so familiar with their surroundings that they can quickly find an escape route or hiding place. And they are sure to notice any change in their surroundings, like a new deer stand. They avoid the area for several days until they get used to the new feature.

Whitetails usually attempt to escape danger by sneaking away unnoticed. When alarmed, bucks and does may snort loudly and stamp their feet. This serves as a warning to other deer. If threatened, a deer bounds away with its snowy white tail or flag, erect. But they normally run only a short distance, then look back to see if they are being pursued. They may stand for many minutes to ascertain if danger is approaching.

A whitetail's coat is reddish brown in spring and summer and brown or gray from fall through winter. Although the underside of the tail is white, the outside is the same color as the rest of the coat and covers up the white rump.

More than two dozen varieties of whitetails inhabit North America. The smallest variety is the Key deer, which generally weighs from 45 to 65 pounds (20 to 29 kg). It lives only in the Florida Keys. Another deer, the Coues whitetail (pronounced "cows"), is found in Arizona, New Mexico and Mexico. It reaches an average live weight of 120 pounds (54 kg) and a shoulder height of 32 inches (81 cm). The largest variety, the northern white-tailed deer, usually weighs from 130 to 190 pounds (58.5 to 85.5 kg). It is found in the northeastern states and into southern Canada. The heaviest whitetail on record, 511 pounds (230 kg), was shot in Minnesota in 1926.

The life span of a whitetail seldom exceeds 8 years. Most deer taken by hunters are 1½ or 2½ years old. You cannot tell a whitetail's age by its antlers. A 1½-year-old buck may have only spikes or it may have three or four points per side. Older bucks usually have four points on a side, but sometimes as many as seven.

The record whitetail rack came from a Saskatchewan deer shot in 1993. Both of the main beams measure 28½ inches (72.4 cm) long. The inside spread is 27¼ inches (69.2 cm). Coues deer have an average antler spread of 11.2 inches (28.5 cm) with a main beam length of 10.6 inches (26.9 cm).

Whitetails can attain speeds of 35 to 40 mph (56 to 64 km/h) and can easily jump an 8-foot (2.4 m) barrier. If they cannot escape by land, they take to water. Whitetails are strong swimmers and have been observed crossing lakes several miles (km) wide.

Shoot for the heart-lung area (red) of a big game animal. The best shot is directly from the side, where the most vital area is exposed. When an animal is quartering toward the hunter, slightly more than half as much vital area is vulnerable; slightly less than half when quartering away. An animal facing the hunter has only a small part of the vital area exposed. Facing away, none of the vital area is vulnerable and the shot would damage too much meat.

Typical antlers are fairly symmetrical, although they sometimes have a different number of tines on each side. But abnormal tines and differences between the two antlers in tine count or size of the main beam lowers the official score of the rack.

Non-typical antlers can be almost symmetrical or extremely asymmetrical. Many have a large number of oddly-shaped tines in unusual locations. Some have tines that point downward. Abnormal points add to the score of non-typical racks.

Whitetails feed primarily on buds and twigs from shrubs and small trees. They also graze on grasses, clover and other green plants. In agricultural areas, they commonly feed on alfalfa, oats, wheat and corn, but eat almost any crop available.

Does spend the summer and fall with one or two fawns. Mature bucks live alone, except during the breeding season. Whitetails mate between October and January. The rutting period lasts longer in the South that it does in the North. During the early stages of the rut, bucks and does become less cautious. Bucks are busy making scrapes to advertise their presence to does. The does move from one scrape to another looking for a suitable mate.

Where to Find Whitetails

No other big game animal has adapted to such a diversity of habitat. Whitetails can be found from the conifer forests of Canada to the chaparral plains of Mexico and from the shoreline of the Atlantic ocean to the river valleys of western Washington and Oregon. The whitetail thrives in farmlands, in suburbs and other areas where human development has severely reduced or eliminated populations of other big game.

Young hardwood forests make prime habitat. Whitetails prefer large woodlands, but can survive in smaller areas like woodlots and tree-lined stream corridors. Deer also live in grasslands, brushlands and swamps.

If you locate a good whitetail area when scouting before the season, chances are the deer will be there when the season begins. Whitetails have a surprisingly small home range. In a Texas study, marked deer were observed over a five-year period. On the average, does remained within a ⅙-square-mile (0.4 sq km) area. Bucks stayed within an area averaging 1⅔ square miles (4.3 sq km).

Your best chance of seeing whitetails is during feeding periods or when they move between resting and feeding areas. Deer feed most heavily before sunrise and after sunset. They bed down in midday. But season, weather, moon phase and hunting pressure can alter daily movements.

The changing seasons can affect whitetail movements in several ways. As the weather begins to cool in fall, deer feed for longer periods to build up their fat reserves for winter. When the acorns start to drop, deer often feed in the woods rather than moving

Scouting for deer continues year-round. Use springtime turkey hunts and early bird seasons to keep track of big game movements and habits.

to their usual feeding areas. Movement increases during the rutting period, as deer wander about in search of a mate.

Changing weather increases deer movement. The animals sense impending weather changes, so they feed heavily while they can. On hot, sunny days, deer spend more time bedded down. They do not necessarily seek cover during a light drizzle. In fact, they often stand out in the open rather than lie in wet grass. But a heavy rain forces them into dense cover.

During a full moon, whitetails may not come out to feed until after dark. In the dark phase, deer begin feeding earlier. They do not feed as heavily at night, because the lack of light curtails their activity.

Hunting pressure can have a dramatic effect on deer movements. In heavily-hunted areas, whitetails change their feeding schedule once the season begins. They feed earlier and later in the day or even at night, to avoid exposing themselves during shooting light.

Rubs on small saplings result from bucks marking their territories by rubbing scent from glands on top of their heads. Bucks rub dozens of trees during the rut, seldom returning to the same ones. They also rub before the rut to remove velvet from their antlers.

Scrapes on the ground mean that a buck is attempting to attract does. As they paw the ground, whitetail bucks often thrash nearby saplings or overhanging branches with their antlers. They check their scrapes regularly, especially those visited by does.

TIPS FOR FINDING WHITETAILS

Tracks and droppings reveal how many deer are using an area. Deer tracks range from $2\frac{1}{2}$ to $3\frac{1}{2}$ inches (5 to 9 cm) long. Whitetail pellets are more elongated than those of rabbits and hares.

Day trails wind through thick brush and trees, but seldom cross clearings. Hunters wait along these trails when deer are most active.

Night trails lead through meadows or open croplands. Do not choose a stand along this type of trail, because deer seldom use them in daylight.

TYPICAL WHITETAIL HABITAT

Hardwood forests provide food and cover. A young forest is best, because sunlight can reach the forest floor to grow shrubs and grasses.

Farmlands offer ample food supplies. They can support large numbers of deer if they have cover like brushy draws or stream corridors.

Lowlands like swamps, bogs and river bottoms provide dense cover. Whitetails usually feed in surrounding fields or woodlands.

HUNTING FOR WHITETAILS

Stand-hunting, still-hunting and driving account for the vast majority of deer taken each year, but hunters use many techniques to outwit whitetails. Antler rattling, stalking, and float-hunting can also be effective.

You can greatly improve your chances by planning your hunt weeks before the season opens. It is possible for an opening-day hunter to leisurely walk into the forest, find a likely-looking spot and bag a trophy buck within minutes. But the odds against such a chance encounter are staggering.

Hunters who enjoy consistent success invest a great deal of time in pre-season scouting. Regardless of how good a spot was in previous years, make sure it still holds good numbers of deer. If you find little sign, look somewhere else. Once you locate a likely area, scout it to determine movement paths and escape routes.

Expert deer hunters know not only where, but when to hunt. Wind is an important consideration. You can approach deer more easily if a light breeze rustles the leaves. This background noise makes the sound of your footsteps less noticeable. In a strong wind, deer bed down in cover and stay extra-alert.

Some hunters prefer a light rain because it softens the leaves and twigs so they do not crackle underfoot. A light rain provides a low level of background noise, but does not reduce deer activity. In a heavy rain, the animals bed down under dense, overhead cover. Powdery snow makes for quiet walking and good tracking. But when a hard crust develops, deer can hear you coming. Snow-covered tree boughs muffle your sound and may block a deer's vision.

Temperature and cloud cover also affect hunting success, but not the way many hunters think. The common belief is that hunting is best on cool or cloudy days. But after thousands of hours of observation, members of a nationwide hunting club found that deer move about more when the weather is warm rather than cold; clear rather than cloudy.

Some hunters use bottled scents, either to mask their own odor or to attract deer. Masking scents are made with skunk or fox urine and sprinkled around the stand. Attractants, made from the urine of a doe in heat or from various fruits, are spread in the area where you want to shoot your deer.

Rattling draws bucks during the rut. Take a stand near a dense thicket where you spotted deer the previous day. Or rattle near a fresh scrape, if the spot offers a clear shot. Rub, knock and rattle two antlers together to imitate the sound of fighting bucks. If nothing appears within 15 to 30 minutes, move quietly to another spot.

You do not need high-velocity cartridges for whitetails, because most shots are at close range. Cartridges should be a minimum of .240 caliber with bullets at least 100 grains.

Stand-hunting for Whitetails

Whitetails are creatures of habit. If you have scouted an area thoroughly and selected a stand near signs of recent deer activity, you can be sure that whitetails will eventually pass your way. If you lose confidence, become impatient and decide to go after the deer, you significantly reduce your odds.

Choose a stand that offers good visibility. It should be located where the wind will not blow your scent toward a trail or other spot where you expect to see deer. You should also select a spot where the sun will not shine in your eyes. Be sure you are concealed on the sides from which deer will most likely approach.

But deer may not come from the direction you expect, so you must slowly scan in a complete circle around your stand. When you spot a deer at a distance, stay motionless and be patient. If you see a doe, watch closely because there may be a buck trailing behind.

If you hunt in the morning, walk to your stand very quietly. Get there while it is still dark. Most hunters stay at their stand until about two hours after sunrise. It often pays to wait a little longer. The commotion caused by other hunters leaving their stands may spook deer to you. If you hunt in the afternoon, stay until the close of shooting hours. Hunters often see more deer in the final minutes than during the rest of the day.

Scouting is critical to the best stand placement. Position a stand to take advantage of daily movements between bedding cover, feed, and water. Ensure that there are clear shooting lanes. On stand, keep your own movements to a minimum and be ready to stay for several hours.

TIPS FOR STAND-HUNTING

Intersections of two or more heavily used trails (left) make prime stand-hunting locations. Anther good spot is an area with many fresh scrapes.

Elevated stands place you above a deer's usual vision level. They also expand your field of view and keep your scent above the ground. But many hunters simply hide behind a tree or a pile of logs or brush.

Raise and lower your unloaded gun or bow with a rope when hunting from an elevated stand. Make sure the barrel is pointed away from you.

Tower blinds make it possible to hunt from a high elevation where there are no tall trees. Some tower blinds are permanent.

Still-hunting for Whitetails

Technology has turned man, the ultimate predator, into man, the consumer. We consume power, petroleum, potato chips, polyester and prescriptions. We run around in circles, from home to school to job to grocery store and home again in the relentless pursuit of more goods to consume. Every year we get better at it, whirling faster and faster.

It is easy to bring our lifestyle to the woods, but it is not welcome there. In fact, it is counter-productive if the goal is to tie a tag on a deer. To succeed, we must become predators again.

The slower you move, the more deer you will see. Place each step carefully; plant your toe first, then gradually lower your heel. Let the sole of your foot feel for a stick

that might snap or gravel that might grind or dry leaves that might crunch. Still hunters should wear shoes or boots with a light sole that allow the hunter to detect noisemakers before they alert game. Stop after a few steps then slowly move your head to examine the terrain. Bend down from time to time to scan the ground below the leaf line.

If you accidentally make a noise, stop. If they do not detect motion, whitetails usually forget the disturbance within a few minutes.

Wait 30 seconds or 1 minute or 5 minutes. Then take another step and scan the woods from this new vantage. You are seeing a new view of the world framed in a different series of trees, looking for the horizontal line of a deer's back or the crook of a leg against the vertical world of trees and brush.

Wind can be a hunter's ally or his worst enemy. Your scent is frightening to most deer. A deer's ability to smell is the one sense that they never question. If the wind is steady from one direction, hunt into it. A steady wind is the friend of the still-hunter.

Successful still-hunting is as much about attitude as it is about stealth. Tell yourself that you will see the deer before they see you. Convince yourself. Believe that the slower you move, the more deer you will see.

Driving for Whitetails

A deer drive's success depends on good organization. A group of hunters wandering haphazardly through the woods has little hope of shooting deer.

Every drive should have a leader who is familiar with the terrain. Before the drive, the leader gives clear instructions to each hunter. Posters take their stands first; each should wait in a spot with a good view, preferably from an elevated stand. Drivers synchronize their watches, then spread out across the upwind side of cover. Distance between the drivers may be only 15 yards (13.7 m) in dense cover or more than 50 yards (45.7 m) if the cover is sparse.

At the appointed time, drivers begin walking downwind. Deer soon detect the hunter's scent. They flush closer if drivers move quietly. Some deer move ahead, some double back and others remain bedded down.

Driving can work anytime deer are in cover. But if you drive a block of cover too large, deer slip to the side and let the drivers pass.

Deer drives can be dangerous. Limit the number of hunters so you can keep track of everyone's location. Posters in elevated stands also make a drive safer. Their shots angle toward the ground and they are above the normal shooting plane of the drivers.

Watch closely for whitetails doubling back through the driving line. Deer may sneak back though drivers are visible on both sides. As drivers approach posters, deer must double back or break into the open.

Keep adjacent drivers in sight at all times. This prevents a hunter from moving too far ahead of the others and into the firing zone.

Post near a known escape route. Deer often move from one block of woods to another by sneaking through a connecting patch of lighter cover.

MULE DEER

The mule deer is named for its long, mule-like ears, but you can tell a mule deer from whitetail by the black tip on its tail. Most of the muley's narrow tail is white, making the rump patch more evident than it is on whitetails. Their antlers also differ. The main beam of a mule deer antler is forked; whitetails have a continuous main beam.

The muley is a much sought-after trophy of the western United States, Canada and Mexico. The record mule deer rack has a spread of 30⅞ inches (78.4 cm). Its right antler has six points and a main beam that measures 30⅛ inches (76.5 cm) long; its left has five points and totals 28¾ inches (73 cm). The animal was shot in Colorado in 1972.

Like whitetails, mule deer have excellent senses of smell and hearing. But muleys have better long-distance vision. They usually bed down where they have a good view of the surrounding terrain. Unlike whitetails, they rarely sit tight and let hunters pass only yards (m) away.

When they detect something unusual, mule deer cock their large ears to pinpoint the direction of the disturbance. Then they bound off in pogo-stick fashion, with all four feet touching the ground simultaneously. This distinctive gait, called stotting, enables them to survey the terrain better and to change direction instantly.

A startled mule deer runs much farther than a whitetail, sometimes up to 4 miles (6.4 km). They usually bound uphill, often pausing for a last look before slipping over a ridge. Muleys normally run with their tails down.

Compared to whitetails, mule deer have a calm disposition. They show little fear of humans as long as enough distance separates them. But they become nervous and often slip away when a hunter disappears from sight.

Mule deer prefer terrain more open than that used by whitetails. Mountains and foothills with sparse stands of timber, rolling prairies broken by canyons and coulees and low brushlands make ideal habitat.

Where mule deer and whitetails co-exist, they eat many of the same foods. But the mule deer's diet usually differs because of the rougher terrain. Common foods include bitterbrush, mountain mahogany, serviceberry, chokecherry and sagebrush. The Pious Report, completed in 1989, found that a mule deer's diet consisted of 55 percent browse (the new growth of trees, shrubs and vines with woody stems), 22 percent forbs (broadleaf plants), 10 percent grasses, 7 percent nuts and 6 percent other materials.

Browse is abundant in mule deer habitat, but broadleaf plants are mule deer favorites. Locate these plants, confirm the deer are eating them and spend time watching in the morning and evening. Early morning and late afternoon are the prime feeding periods. Favorite areas are brushy hillsides, meadows, croplands and pastures, generally at lower elevations than bedding areas.

Mule deer move as much as 2 miles (3.2 km) from feeding to bedding areas. In midday, they often bed down on the lee side of a break. They may rest just below the crest of a hill or the lip of a ravine. They watch only the downhill side, relying on the wind to bring them the scent of anything approaching from behind. Mule deer also bed on grassy mountain terrain, in the bottom of a dry wash or near a tree on a hillside. In remote areas, they may feed in the open rather than bed down during the day.

Daily movements usually begin with mule deer moving to feeding areas like a grassy stream margin in a ravine. They feed until 1 to 2 hours after sunrise, then bed in areas like a ledge near the top of the ravine. Large bucks may bed on rocky terraces at higher elevation. Deer return to feeding areas about an hour before sunset.

Deer take their water from ponds, puddles, creeks, rivers, lakes, seeps and succulent plants. Researchers in another study found that they travel an average of 800 yards (731 m) to get it. They approach, ever watchful for predators, because coyotes, cougar and other carnivores need water too.

After a rainy period, look for mule deer on sunny hillsides. Heavy snow drives them from the mountains to lower ground. Herds migrate as far as 50 miles (80 km), often wintering in brushy draws and canyons that are blown free of snow.

Mule deer often form large herds, especially during the breeding season. Small and medium-sized bucks mix with does and fawns, but the largest bucks are usually loners.

Most mule deer breed in November and December, but the breeding period may be as early as October or as last as March. During the rut, the bucks thrash or horn bushes, poles, branches and tree trunks in a display of dominance. They do not make scrapes.

Seven varieties of mule deer inhabit the western third of North America. The desert mule deer ranges as far south as central Mexico. The most numerous variety,

the Rocky Mountain mule deer, is found as far north as the Northwest Territories.

Rocky Mountain mule deer reach the largest size, generally weighing from 140 to 200 pounds (63 to 90 kg). The largest on record, 453 pounds (203.85 kg), was taken in Montana. The southern mule deer is the smallest variety; it weighs from 85 to 110 pounds (38.25 to 49.5 kg).

Hunting for Mule Deer

Mule deer live in rugged mountainous terrain and high desert landscapes. They may feed in the valley on a rancher's alfalfa, but they most often bed on the high ground where they can spot danger a long way off.

A mule deer's survival strategy includes identifying the predator, then putting distance and obstacles between himself and danger. Many hunters have scored on a buck because it stopped to take one last look before it went out of sight. Some make the mistake of thinking that mule deer are easier to outsmart than whitetails, but the truth is a big mule deer is one of the most sought-after trophies on the continent.

Mule deer hunting in open country lends itself to the spot-and-stalk method. Get to the highest part of your hunting area early in the morning, preferably before shooting light. The chances of spotting muleys in the open are best in the morning and the evening. The high elevation affords a good view.

Glass every detail of the landscape, first with binoculars then with a spotting scope. Mule deer blend in well with their surroundings and are masters at concealment in a small amount of cover. Sometimes it takes movement of the sun and shadow to reveal a feeding or bedded animal. If you spot one deer, look closely for others because mule deer often feed and bed in groups.

Glass potential feeding and bedding areas with binoculars. A spotting scope works better for long distances. Look for a reflection off shiny antlers; buff-white patches of throat or rump hair; or the symmetrical shape of a mule deer's face and ears, which resembles a three-bladed propeller.

If the animal is too far away for a shot, plan a stalk. Have a partner stay at the spotting scope and direct the approach using hand signals. Use natural features of the landscape, like ravines, for concealment. Try to approach from downwind and above, because muleys expect danger from below.

Should glassing prove futile, still-hunt your way downhill. Some hunters take stands along trails where muleys are likely to pass on the way to bed, feed or water. When hunting with companions, driving can be effective.

A running buck makes a difficult target because of its stotting gait and unpredictable turns. But it may stop and look back if you shout, whistle or make a deer call.

Mule deer hunters take shots at up to 300 yards (274 m), so sight in your rifle for long-range shooting. Use a high-velocity cartridge of at least .240 caliber with a minimum bullet weight of 95 grains.

Still-hunt a series of ravines by starting at the head of one ravine, then walking the edge. Look over the crest periodically to spot bedded deer. Cross the ravine at the lower end and walk the other side to check for deer you may have missed. Then, cross to the head of the next ravine and repeat the procedure.

Stand-hunt along corridors between feeding and bedding areas. Conceal yourself behind a natural feature like a rock outcrop or large tree or use a tree stand. Mule deer trails are usually less distinct than those of whitetails. But the animals often follow natural passes like a saddle between two ridges.

HOW TO DRIVE FOR MULE DEER

Drive for mule deer in ravines. One hunter walks up the bottom and another halfway up the side. A third hunter posts at the head of the ravine. Driving also works well along wooded or brushy stream corridors.

Never shoot at a deer when it is on top of a ridge. Always be sure there is a solid backstop behind the animal before shooting. Bullets travel completely through them.

BLACK-TAILED DEER

Due in part to their narrow geographic range, black-tailed deer are largely ignored in the popular hunting press, but this animal is one of America's most prized trophies. Blacktails are a subspecies of mule deer and their territories overlap along the eastern boundaries of the smaller deer's range. A doe weighs 70 to 140 pounds (30 to 66 kg). Bucks weigh between 120 and 250 pounds (57 to 120 kg). A buck may measure up to 36 inches (90 cm) at the shoulder.

Antler growth is similar to mule deer. Males grow branching tined antlers. Typical antlers are four-points (western count), but many blacktails mature with three-points per side (not counting eye guards).

They are called blacktails because the bottom two-thirds of the tail is black. The tail is wider than a mule deer's tail. At the base, it is brown. The underside is white. Blacktails are reddish-brown in the summer and tend to go gray-brown in the fall.

Black-tailed deer can be found throughout western Canada, western Washington, western Oregon and northern California, but certain types of habitat hold them in greater numbers. If you want to see blacktails, watch clearcuts and burns. Logging benefits these animals because it opens up the forest canopy to let in the sunshine. New growth springs up and deer can find most of what they need all in one place.

Deer need food, water, shelter and space. Sometimes they get all four in a clearcut. They also become vulnerable to hunters. That's why you only find does, fawns and immature bucks in large openings.

If you want to fill your tag with a doe (when legal) or a young buck, hunt the clearcuts in the morning, bedding areas at noon and paths leading from bedding areas in late afternoon. You will find the deer.

However, clearcuts are not as easy to find as they once were. Now, chemicals are used to control weeds, what we hunters refer to as forbs and what deer call groceries. Today's super-fast-growing tree seedlings turn clearcuts into tall timber again, a lot faster than they used to. Also, fear of fire may keep gates closed to timber company lands in low-water years, with "No Access" signs posted until the rains come.

It doesn't take much habitat to hide a deer, and many big blacktail bucks grow old without ever being seen by a hunter. Their sanctuaries provide both cover and food. Water can be reached after dark. During the general rifle season, bucks may spend most of their time in an area of just a few acres (ha).

In open country and oak savannah, black-tailed deer are vulnerable to spot-and-stalk tactics. Take up a position before first light and employ a spotting scope to cover a lot of distance from one place. An afternoon stand can pay off with a glimpse of a big buck right before dark.

WHERE TO FIND BLACKTAILS

A good strategy is to look for the pockets the crowds pass by. Sometimes they may be so obvious that no one would think to hunt there. Sometimes they are so far back in the timber or the brush is so thick that other hunters detour around it.

In oak savannah, the hills are often bare, especially the south-facing exposures. Blackberry bushes, poison oak, oak trees and scattered pines grow up the sides, with bedding cover found in the run-off washes and along the creek bottoms. Old road beds provide dependable travel corridors and trails are visible from hundreds of yards (meters) away, showing where a hunter might expect to see a deer emerge from the heavy cover.

Deer are easily seen from the tops of the hills, but usually, glimpses of does and forked horns are the pay-off. Wiser bucks know to bed in the sticker patches when the orange-clad horde takes to the ridges. The bigger bucks have seen it all before.

Finding Unpressured Deer in Pockets of Cover

To find pockets that other people pass by, use a 7.5 Minute Series, 1:24000 U.S. Geological Survey map. With the contour intervals of 40 feet (12 m) on a 7.5 minute topo, it's easy to pinpoint roadless areas, identify swamps, spot north-facing ridges and locate most of the springs and seeps. You can also identify escape routes and make an estimate at where to find the dense cover where deer bed.

In these hideouts, most big black-tailed bucks grow old without ever being seen by a hunter. Their sanctuaries provide both cover and food. Water can be reached after dark. During the general rifle season, bucks spend most of their time in an area of just a few acres (ha) and feed after the sun goes down.

Private land may be the key to access, even to public ground. Get permission to cross a neighbor's land. If parking pull-outs are few and far between, have someone drop you off along the road. If a stream is the boundary, use waders or float a boat. Whatever it takes, hunt the ground other hunters can't or won't get to. And don't fall into their patterns.

Mature blacktails seldom come easy. Examine aerial photos and topo maps to find the places where the big boys live. Locate natural escape routes such as saddles and canyons. Look for brushy shelves where a buck can watch his backtrail from his bed. Locate a trail from a nearby feeding area or water and you have found a buck's living room.

Hunt into the wind and watch every step. Move too fast and deer will see you before you spot them. Slow down. Every time you take a step, a new window opens in the heavy cover. Look for the horizontal line of a back, the black of a nose, the flick of a tail, the crook of a leg or sunlight glinting from a nut-brown antler. Carry binoculars on a harness against your chest, not in a daypack. And use them.

Learning to recognize feed, water, bedding ground and escape cover are the fundamentals of hunting these most challenging of our western deer.

Carry your lunch and stay in the woods all day. Watch a trail leading into a bedding area and let other hunters push the deer your way. In the timber, hunt from above, whether from a tree stand or looking down from a high cliff. Such stands afford greater visibility, keep you above the line of sight and keep your scent stream above the game.

In open country, use a spotting scope to scout bucks on distant hilltops. It's always better to see them first and plan a strategy.

When scouting for blacktails, think small. A strip of trees between roads can hold a deer. A half-acre (0.2 ha) behind the barn may hold a buck, as will an island in a river or a lake. You may find such a spot anywhere in blacktail country.

Black-tailed deer are among the most wary of all big game animals. Learn their habits, their preferred foods, and their bedding areas. Scouting pays off with more deer sightings during the season.

ELK

Sought after and prized for its magnificent antlers and savory meat, a mature bull elk is the big game hunter's greatest trophy. A large animal may have antlers 5 feet (1.5 m) long.

Antlers of the largest bulls, called monarchs, have eight points on a side. Imperial elk have seven points per side and royal elk six. The record elk rack has eight points on one side and seven on the other. The main beam of one antler measures 59⅛ inches (151.5 cm); the other 55⅝ inches (141.3 cm). The rack, which has a 45½ inch (115.5 cm) spread, came from an elk taken in Colorado in 1899.

Two varieties of elk provide the vast majority of hunting. Most numerous is the Rocky Mountain elk. The slightly larger Roosevelt elk lives in the coastal mountains of the Pacific Northwest. Elk are brownish-gray with long, chestnut-brown hair on the neck. The tail and rump patch are buff-white. Bulls average about 750 pounds (337.5 kg) and stand 5 feet (1.5 m) high at the shoulder. Cows weigh about one-fourth less. The smaller tule elk are found in California.

Elk prefer heavily timbered country broken by clearcuts, burns and meadows. The best habitat is in remote, mountainous terrain laced with streams and small glacial lakes. Elk also make their home in desert environs. In dry country, elk have large territories and do not tolerate human disturbance.

Cow elk live in large herds which also include calves and an occasional spike bull. An old cow leads the herd, alerting the others to danger with a sharp bark. Older bulls live alone or in small groups of up to six. Bulls wander more than cows, shunning cow herds until the mating season.

The breeding season or rut begins sometime between late August and mid-September. Bulls break out of their summer bachelor herds and locate on ridgelines. A dominant bull, called a herd bull, bugles to advertise for a harem that may number up to 30 cows. He protects them from the advances of younger males, also called satellites or of other herd bulls.

To detect danger, elk rely mainly on a keen sense of smell. They also have excellent hearing. On windy days, when swishing tree limbs would obscure the sound of a hunter's approach, they become nervous and retreat to heavy cover. Elk quickly notice movement, but usually ignore stationary objects.

An elk can run 35 mph (56 km/h) in a short burst and can maintain a 15 to 20 mph (24 to 32 km/h) trot over a long distance. A running bull carries his nose high, so his antlers lay back along his body and do not tangle in branches. Elk are strong swimmers and can jump obstructions up to 10 feet high (3 m).

Elk feed mainly on grasses. As winter nears, they browse on twigs and leaves from shrubs and trees. The morning feeding period begins about one hour before sunrise and lasts until one hour after. In late afternoon, they begin feeding about two hours before sunset and continue until dark. Elk usually have four or five shorter feeding periods during the day, each lasting from 15 minutes to one hour. Because they eat so often, elk usually bed within 1 mile (1.6 km) of where they feed. They prefer bedding areas with a good view, like a grassy terrace or bench about half of the way up on a hillside.

In summer and early fall, elk scatter over a large area at high elevation. The rugged terrain prevents intrusion by humans. In late fall, heavy snow and extreme cold push elk to lower elevations. But with a break in the

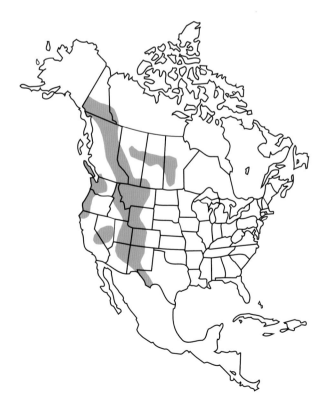

weather, they may return to high altitudes. Some herds move 100 miles (161 km) to find the right conditions.

Daily movement patterns depend on hunting pressure. When not disturbed, elk feed in open meadows or areas with young trees and shrubs. They bed down at the edge of timber nearby. If threatened, they move up to 5 miles (8 km) into the timber after feeding. Or they may retreat to a steep, conifer-studded slope where they sniff rising air currents to detect danger from below.

Migrations in late fall begin when snow depth reaches 19 inches (48.25 cm) or more and temperatures plunge below zero Fahrenheit (–17°C). Elk move to snow-free, south-facing slopes at lower elevations.

Bugling consists of a series of melodious whistles, progressing from a low to high pitch. Herd bulls bugle to intimidate competing males. Challengers bugle and chuckle to lure the herd bull away from his harem. In addition to bugling, herd bulls bellow, rake trees with their antlers, display and spar with other bulls to drive them off. Occasionally, two bulls fight each other in a test of strength.

SIGNS OF ELK ACTIVITY

Droppings that are elongated and ¾ to 1½ inches (1.9 to 3.8 cm) in length mean that elk have been browsing on twigs and leaves. Droppings in a large mass are from elk that have eaten green grass.

Wallows are made by big bulls to announce their presence to cows. A bull scrapes out a depression at a spring seep. He urinates in the mud, then rolls in it, plastering his body.

Fresh rubs during the rut also advertise a large bull's presence. Elk rubs are higher than those made by deer and the bark of the sapling is stripped over a greater length.

Hunting for Elk

A successful elk hunter must earn his or her trophy. Unlike most other big game animals, elk retreat deep into the forest or climb to extreme elevations to escape hunting pressure.

Plan to spend several days on the hunt. Scout a prospective area to find fresh elk sign, then set up camp at least 1 mile (1.6 km) away.

Scent can help you locate areas used by elk. The animals emit a strong, musky odor. The scent lingers in bedding or wallowing areas long after the elk leave.

One of the most productive techniques is stand-hunting in early morning and late afternoon, especially when the stand is on or near a saddle that the elk use to move between one drainage and the next. For a morning hunt, walk to your stand in the dark, moving quietly to avoid spooking any elk in the vicinity. Remain on your stand until about two hours after sunrise, glassing to find elk that you could stalk. In the afternoon, be on your stand at least two hours before sunset.

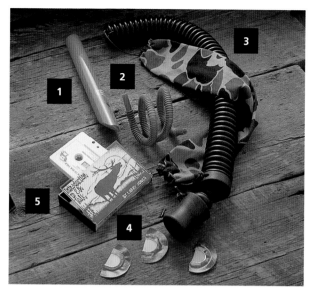

Calls include: (1) flute, (2) pigtail and (3) tube types. Diaphragm calls (4) mimic small, medium and old bulls. Tapes, CDs and DVDs (5) help you learn the best calls.

In midday, when elk are bedded down, you are more likely to see them by still-hunting. The technique works best when the ground is damp or covered with soft snow. Noise doesn't spook the elk as much as scent does. Use scent control to keep the human odor in check.

Driving can be effective, but only if the hunting party is familiar with the terrain. Drivers approach from below a known bedding area and push the elk uphill to posters. The posters station themselves along game trails in thick timber or near clearings where elk are likely to break into the open. Startled elk make plenty of noise. But more often, they slip away silently, so posters must watch closely.

During the rut, hunters can bugle in bull elk. Many elk calls mimic the high-pitched, squeaky whistle of a spike bull. This call infuriates the herd bull. He thinks an unworthy youngster is making a play for his harem, so he moves toward the caller, ready to do battle. If a bull answers but does not move, he is probably guarding his harem and reluctant to leave. In this case, try stalking close enough for a shot.

Because elk are so large and shooting distances so long, most hunters prefer high-velocity cartridges of .270 caliber or larger. Use a bullet weighing at least 150 grains.

A bow hunter should use a bow set up with a pull weight of at least 50 pounds (22.5 kg) and a razor-sharp, strong, fixed-blade broadhead. Muzzleloader hunters are best equipped when using a .50-caliber or larger, stoked with a premium bullet.

Pack trains enable hunters to reach the remote, mountainous areas which offer the best elk hunting. Horses or mules also simplify the task of carrying out the antlers and cut-up carcasses.

Bugle for elk starting at dawn. When a bull answers, move toward him, staying downwind and calling about every five minutes as long as he continues to respond. Keep approaching until you get within about 400 yards (366 m). Then, select a blind and continue calling to lure him within shooting range.

Stand-hunt above trails or wallows or at the edge of a meadow where elk feed. Trails and feeding areas are most productive in early morning and late afternoon. Bulls usually visit wallows late in the day.

OTHER ELK HUNTING TECHNIQUES

Still-hunt to within shooting range. Bowhunters often get as close as 20 yards (18 m). Start by walking a ridge, looking for elk on terraces or hillsides. Approach elk from above because they usually watch the downhill side.

Follow fresh elk tracks in the snow. The tracks generally measure 3½ to 5 inches (9 to 13 cm). Stay on the trail as long as it goes downhill; stay above the trail if it moves across the slope. Constantly look ahead so you see the animal before it sees you.

MOOSE

Most hunters are awestruck by the sight of their first bull moose.

With antlers towering 10 feet (3 m) above the ground, a bull moose is truly a magnificent sight. A large bull weighs 1,200 pounds (540 kg) and moose up to 1,800 pounds (810 kg) have been recorded. The world-record rack has a 65⅛-inch (165.4 cm) spread. The right palm measures 54½ inches (138.4 cm) and has 19 points; the left 53¾ inches (136.5 cm) with 15 points.

Like other members of the deer family, moose have an excellent sense of smell and good hearing. But their eyesight is poorer than that of deer. Moose seldom notice a nearby hunter if he or she does not move.

Despite their size, moose can run up to 30 mph (50.8 km/h). When spooked, they crash through brush and small trees, ignoring trails. But moose can also slip quietly through cover to elude a hunter.

Young hardwood forests with scattered conifers and brushy lowlands make ideal moose habitat. The dense undergrowth provides ample food and bedding cover. But they can also live in older forests with little underbrush.

A big bull can browse on vegetation up to 11 feet (3.35 m) off the ground. If it cannot reach the upper portion of a small tree, a moose straddles the trunk, then starts walking. The animal bends down the tree, feeding on leaves and twigs as it walks. Moose feed most heavily from just before sunrise to about two hours after, and again in late afternoon. But they may feed anytime during the day or night. When not feeding, moose bed down in the thickets.

Most of the year, moose live by themselves. They lead docile lives, seldom moving more than ½ mile (0.8 km/h) in a day, but during the rut, which begins in September, bulls become ill-tempered. They have been known to attack cars and even trains. Rutting bulls regularly visit wallows. Both sexes roam widely during the rut, sometimes wandering over 10 miles (16 km) from their usual home range.

Hunters see the most moose on clear, calm days. Heavy overcast, rain, snow or high winds keep the animals bedded down.

Before you hunt, scout the area for sign. With animals of this size, the evidence will be obvious. Select a stand near a wallow, a well-used stream crossing or any spot where the topography funnels moose through a small area. Get to your stand before daylight, remain until mid-morning, then return in late afternoon.

Still-hunting can be effective at midday, especially if there is snow to quiet your footsteps. If you attempt to sneak through heavy timber and brush, you will make too much noise. During the rut, antler rattling or calling may lure bulls from dense cover. Using cupped hands or a birchbark megaphone, make a series of short grunts to imitate a cow in heat. If you hear a response, pour water in a puddle to imitate a cow urinating.

In hilly or mountainous country, hunters stalk moose after spotting them with binoculars. Float-hunting works well along streams and lakeshores.

Most moose hunters use large-caliber rifles and high-velocity ammunition, similar to those used for elk. A moose may not drop immediately after the shot. To prevent losing a wounded animal, wait 10 to 15 minutes for it to lie down, then begin to track it.

Moose have a dark brown, almost black, coat. A large bull stands 7 feet (2 m) tall at the shoulder and measures 10 feet (3 m) in length. Each antler has a large palm with numerous points along the outer edge. Moose usually stay near water. Bogs and lakes provide a source of food, a place to cool off and a refuge from swarms of insects. Excellent swimmers, moose will not hesitate to cross a fast river or even a large lake. Moose tracks measure about 5 to 7 inches (13 to 18 cm) long.

TIPS FOR FINDING MOOSE

Broken saplings indicate a bull moose in rut. A bull twists off saplings with his antlers to advertise his presence to cows.

Droppings measure 1 to 1½ inches (2.5 to 3.8 cm) long. When moose are eating browse, droppings have a consistency similar to compressed sawdust.

Brushy lowlands are favorite feeding areas. Moose prefer red-osier dogwood, willow, aspen, birch, mountain ash and aquatic plants.

MOOSE HUNTING TECHNIQUES

Glass for moose along forest edges, in willow swamps or near other feeding areas. Get to your vantage point early, so you can complete your stalk before the animals retreat to bedding areas.

Float-hunt for moose if preliminary scouting shows abundant sign along the stream bank. The technique works best in early morning and late afternoon, when moose come to drink and to feed on shoreline willows.

PRONGHORN

The fleet-footed pronghorn can reach a speed of 60 mph (96.5 km/h), unmatched among North American big game animals. According to fossil records, they are the only true native big game species on the North American continent. It is thought that all other big game are descended from animals that crossed the Bering Strait from Asia.

Hunters refer to pronghorns as antelope but they are not related to the antelope of Africa. Pronghorns get their name from the sharp prongs that project forward on the horns of bucks. Their upper body is tan; the underside and rump white. The record pronghorn rack has a right horn measuring 17¾ inches (45.1 cm) in length. Its left horn totals 17¼ inches (43.8 cm) long. The animal was shot in Arizona in 1985.

Special adaptations for stamina such as an oversized windpipe and large lung capacity compared to their body size enable pronghorns to maintain high speeds for several miles (km). Their large eyeballs are approximately 2 inches (5 cm) in diameter and their vision is unequaled.

Pronghorns prefer open plains, prairies and treeless foothills. The best habitat has rolling hills sprinkled with water holes and ample sagebrush for food. One study showed that the typical diet consisted of 55 percent sagebrush, 30 percent rabbitbrush, 7 percent grass and 5 percent forbs (broadleaf plants). They feed most heavily in early morning and late afternoon, but may graze anytime day or night. During the spring and early summer pronghorns get most of their water needs met from succulent vegetation in their diet, but in the dry seasons of midsummer and fall they go to a water hole at least once a day.

This animal is wary and nervous and constantly on the lookout for any signs of danger. The pronghorn's sense of smell is good; however, sight and speed are their primary defenses. When alarmed, an antelope flares its white rump hairs or makes a barking sound, alerting others in the herd. Contrary, however, to their skittish nature, pronghorns are remarkably curious and may move a considerable distance to investigate an unusual sight.

Most antelope weigh 80 to 130 pounds (36 to 58.5 kg), with the largest bucks weighing up to 140 (63 kg).

The breeding season begins in August in northern pronghorn range and may occur as late as November in the south. In spring, mature dominant bucks claim territories that contain the best food and water. They vigorously defend the territory against other intruding bucks. As the rut approaches, the dominant or herd buck attempts to gather and keep a large harem of does in his territory, breeding each when they come into estrus. Pronghorn buck fights, as the herd buck chases intruding bucks away, seldom result in serious injury. These distractions can last long enough for a hunter to stalk within range.

Spot-and-stalk is the primary tactic when hunting pronghorns. The hunter glasses, with binoculars or a spotting scope, from a high point of ground. After a good buck is spotted, a stalk, utilizing any available cover, is planned to get within shooting range.

Stand-hunting tactics can be used if a herd shows repeated daily movement patterns. Some hunters set up a blind and wait near a well-used waterhole or fence crossing. Pronghorns prefer to go under or through fences. They habitually cross at the same places, leaving hair on the barbed wire or on the ground. Stand-hunting near these locations is often productive.

Most hunters opt for a flat-shooting rifle, but using the contour of the land a gun hunter may be able to approach within 100 yards (91 m). Bowhunters must get much closer and have developed methods to overcome the limited range of their weapons. Decoying can be an effective method when the bucks are rutting. The hunter puts up the decoy within sight of a dominant buck, hiding behind it, hoping that the antelope will challenge this intruder. Antelope calls may also be used, when decoying, to challenge aggressive bucks. Calls may be used by a gun hunter.

TIPS FOR HUNTING PRONGHORN

Identify bucks by their black cheek patch. Mature bucks have horns that extend above the ears. Some does have buttons or spikes, but they are shorter than the ears.

Challenge a rutting buck during the archery season using a decoy. Never use a decoy during gun season.

Stand-hunt from a blind near a water hole or fence crossing. Or simply hide in a depression.

BLACK BEAR

The complete hunter not only hunts for deer, elk, caribou and moose, but does his or her part to control predator populations. Spring and fall bear hunts offer another chance to pursue your passion.

The black bear is a predator and an omnivore. To some it is a pest, to others a trophy. To all it is an icon of wilderness and wild country. Of all big game animals, bear are the most misunderstood. Black bear are dangerous game because they are unpredictable.

Black bear favor a habitat of mixed conifers and hardwoods, with clearings that produce food. A bear's diet consists mainly of berries, fruits, nuts, grasses and crops. They also eat insects, small and large mammals and fish. In spring, they may feed on carcasses of animals killed by severe winter weather. Bear have an enormous appetite in late summer and fall. A mature boar can gain over 100 pounds (45 kg) in preparation for hibernation.

Bear feed most heavily during cool morning and evening hours. They remain in the shade on hot days because their fur absorbs too much heat from the sun. Windy or rainy weather limits their activity.

With the exception of the June breeding season, males or boars, lead solitary lives. Sows stay with cubs for about 1½ years. Boars have a much larger territory than sows, often over 100 square miles (260 sq km).

They may go into hibernation between October and December depending on the latitude and weather conditions. They remain in their dens until April, although they occasionally wander about during a warm spell. In warmer climates, bear may not hibernate. If they do, hibernation begins later and does not last as long.

Black bear come in color phases. Most are glossy black, brown or cinnamon, but they may be white or even bluish. A large boar weighs 300 to 400 pounds (135 to 180 kg); some exceed 600 (270 kg). Sows weigh about one-third less. The largest black bear on record weighed 802 pounds (360.9 kg). It was taken in Wisconsin in 1885.

Biologists rate the bear among the most intelligent game animals. A bear can run 25 mph (40 km/h) and climb a tree in seconds. They rely mainly on a keen sense of smell to find food and detect danger. They have excellent hearing and fair eyesight.

Even in good bear country, the animals are not abundant, averaging only one bear for every 2 square miles (5.2 sq km). Because bear are scattered, hunters employ techniques seldom used for other big game.

To many, the music of a pack of hunting hounds is what the chase is about. Walkers, black-and-tans or Plotts are most often employed for bear hunting. A bear can run for miles (km) and often loses the dogs. When cornered, it can quickly kill or injure a hound. Some hunters pursue bear solely for the sport of the chase. Once an animal is treed or brought to bay, they call off the dogs and let it go.

Others like the intrigue and challenge of luring a bear with baits. Baiting takes advantage of the bear's highly developed sense of smell. A bear can detect the scent of bait at up to 3 miles (4.8 km) away. This method works in spring when hungry bear emerge from dens and in fall when they feed heavily to build up fat reserves.

Patient spot-and-stalk hunting pays off where the use of dogs or bait is illegal. Hunters choose a canyon where they can watch the edge of a meadow or a patch of berries to spot feeding bears.

Calling works as well. A rodent or a fawn-in-distress call can bring in a hungry or curious bear. Use an electronic call to bring the bear within range. Let the call play constantly for up to an hour or more.

In some regions, damage complaints from bears are at an all-time high. Wildlife biologists have fewer tools today to deal with problem bears. The biologist's best friend is the hunter who has mastered the art of hunting the black bear.

Bear hunters use rifles of at least .30 caliber and bullets that weigh at least 165 grains (10.7 gm). You can kill a bear with a smaller caliber, but a larger caliber is most effective.

If there's one thing a hungry bear wants more than anything else, it's an easy meal. And he's used to taking food away from smaller predators. Black bear will come to a call, but bears have a short attention span. On the way in, he may stumble across a berry patch or a spawning salmon. Keep the sound rolling to keep him on the move. And give him time. Depending on how far he's got to travel, you may see the bruin in a few minutes or an hour. Keep the wind in your favor and your confidence high. Commit to spending an hour at each call set.

TIPS FOR FINDING BEARS

Tracks (left) have distinct claw marks and measure 3½ to 5 inches (9 to 12.7 cm) wide. The front foot is 4 to 5 inches (10 to 12.7 cm) long; the hind foot 6 to 7 inches (15.25 to 17.75 cm).

Damaged trees or bushes are common feeding signs. A bear rips down a branch with its claws, then strips off the fruit or berries.

Droppings reveal what bear have been eating. They often contain berries, grass, hair and wood eaten along with insects.

Bait black bear with food scraps. Cover each bait station with logs to keep out smaller scavengers. Bait several different locations before the season, then select a stand near a bait-site that bear visit regularly.

Follow hounds on foot or horseback until they tree or corner a bear. Hunters scout a potential area to locate fresh tracks, then release the dogs. Even if the scent is cold, good dogs pick up the bear's trail.

WILD BOAR

The Spanish brought the first domestic hogs to California in the sixteenth century. Today, their descendants can be hunted in many places in the South and in California and other western states.

This isn't your average agricultural species. Adult wild hogs tip the scales between 100 and 200 pounds (45 and 90 kg). Boars can reach 375 (169 kg). Most European/feral crosses have a coat of long, coarse, dark hair. Boars grow wicked tusks and are not the kind of animals you'd like to run into on a narrow trail.

Wild hogs come in all shapes and sizes. Long, coarse, dark hair is a characteristic of wild swine, wherever they are found. The ears are small, erect and hairy and tufted at the tips. Tails are long, straight and mule-like, in comparison with domestic pigs. They are lean, with shoulders higher and wider than their hindquarters. A wild boar may stand up to 35 inches (89 cm) at the shoulder. Wild hogs also have longer snouts than domestic swine and longer, sharper tusks (up to about 3 inches/7.6 cm in length).

Wild hogs are also faster runners than their farm-bound kin. They can hit speeds of up to 35 mph (56 km/h).

In periods between rains, you can scout for hogs at watering holes and fresh wallows. Such places will be visited by hogs at least once a day. A word of warning—bag your boar before he's all covered with fresh mud.

They eat everything from acorns to alfalfa, to rattlesnakes and bird eggs. And they multiply. Starting at six months old, a sow can produce piglets at the rate of two litters per year.

There is no limit on hogs in many states. You need a hunting license and you may need a tag. And all your hunting skill.

Spot-and-Stalk for Swine

A spotting scope can help locate hogs, but often, binoculars are all you'll need. You can watch from one vantage point or move from hill to hill. Your best bet is in the first hour and the last hour of the day. Generally, the herd is bedded down for the day, but may get up to move around a little at noon.

Feeding swine don't stay in one place very long. If you spot animals a long way out, watch them long enough to get an idea where they're headed. Then meet them there.

For two or more hunters, it's often better to split up to cover more ground. But hunting should be conducted in a low-impact manner. Stay on roads and established trails and out of bedding areas. Spook the herd and they're likely to leave the area or go nocturnal. When you crest a hill, go easy. Take a few steps then glass the habitat that has just opened up to view.

Hogs aren't known for superior visual acuity, but too often hunters don't give a hog's eyes enough credit. As much as possible, use the terrain and the cover of the trees to get in close enough for a shot.

Wind direction is the biggest consideration. Let them smell you and those hogs will be heading for cover in a hurry. Better to constantly check the way the breeze is blowing and plan your hunt and your stalks to keep the wind in your face.

Hogs are creatures of habit. The same trails are used day after day, season after season, dependent on the food sources. In ranchland, you'll see dozens of broad trails leading from bedding areas to feeding areas. You'll find coarse black hair on the barbs of a fence and deep split-toed tracks at watering areas. Choose a stand where you can keep track of two or more trails at once.

In periods between rains, scout for fresh wallows. Such places are visited by hogs at least once a day.

Guns and Loads for Wild Boar

The wild boar is not easy to kill. It has a tough shoulder hide called a shield that protects it from thorns. Your bullet must penetrate this armor and retain enough energy to destroy the heart or lungs. Often the hog doesn't drop at the first shot.

Many shots have to be taken on the run. A well-balanced rifle can help you get on target fast. Keep the scope dialed down to 3× for quick acquisition of the target. Many hunters choose a 30-caliber like the .308 or the .30-06 while handgun hunters prefer the 44 Magnum.

TYPICAL BOAR BIOLOGY

Males and females both have tusks. They may grow to 5 to 9 inches (13 to 23 cm) long.

Wild hogs have a split toe (right). Large hogs leave the imprint of both the hooves and the dew claws.

SIGNS OF WILD BOAR ACTIVITY

Wallows (left) are used by hogs to coat themselves with mud to keep insects at bay. Look for tracks around water holes and the presence of stirred-up mud in the water.

Two signs of hog activity: rooting for grubs and dried mud on the side of the tree where a big boar scratched.

Between rains, hogs head for water every day. Look for tracks around water holes.

Chapter 5

HUNTING SMALL GAME

The popularity of small game hunting stems from the relative ease of finding game and access. With a little scouting, you can probably locate rabbits, squirrels, raccoons or woodchucks within a few miles (km) of your home. Even with a minimum of equipment, you can find great sport and bring home a tasty meal.

Even the novice has a reasonable chance of bagging rabbits or squirrels. But this does not mean that small game hunting is easy. Your success will improve as your level of skill increases. You can apply the skills you gain to other types of hunting.

Small game hunters have many opportunities to enjoy their sport. Most hunting seasons last at least six months and some are continuous. Because you can find these animals close to home, you can make frequent short trips, which is difficult when hunting most other types of game. Almost all states and provinces have liberal bag limits.

Most hunters use shotguns or rimfire rifles chambered at .17 or .22 caliber. But some prefer a combination gun with a .22 caliber rifle barrel on top and a 20-gauge shotgun barrel on the bottom. Combination guns are ideal for small game because you can fire one barrel at standing animals and the other at running targets. Other hunters employ handguns to bring home the game. You can also use small-caliber center-fire rifles, muzzleloading rifles, shotguns and bows with blunt-tipped arrows.

A pair of waterproof leather boots is a good investment. With the possible exceptions of brush pants, a burr-proof jacket with a game pouch, binoculars and a small knife for field dressing, you need little other equipment.

Many hunters compare rabbit and squirrel meat to chicken. Raccoon tends to be oily and has a distinctive flavor of its own. Small game tastes better if you remove the entrails soon after killing the animal.

COTTONTAIL RABBIT

Rabbits don't require a lot to thrive: a little food, water, shelter and escape cover. They can find everything they need in a few acres (ha) of ground. Best of all, rabbits may be hunted close to home.

Each year, hunters throughout North America bag more than 40 million cottontail rabbits. This staggering total results from the cottontail's tremendous reproductive rate and its ability to adapt to a wide range of habitats and foods.

Cottontails breed in the spring and summer, producing up to eight litters, each with three to six young. They prefer brushy edges and woodlots, but can live almost anywhere, with the exception of dense forests. They eat practically any type of green plant. When green vegetation dies back, they switch to twigs and bark.

Rabbits start feeding before dawn and continue for two or three hours. They resume feeding at sunset. They move about most on calm, sunny days. Rain or wind drives them into heavy cover.

A cottontail spends most of the day sitting in a form, a shallow depression in grass or snow. The grass eventually wears away or the snow melts down and compacts. Often a form is concealed by overhanging grass or other type of overhead cover.

Rabbits use their superb hearing to sense impending danger. To escape, they bolt away on established travel lanes. Cottontails run in an elusive, zig-zag pattern, but their speed is not as fast as a jackrabbit. They average 12 to 15 mph (19 to 24 km/h), but can reach 20 mph (32 km/h).

Normally, cottontails do not run far. Rather than run straight away, a rabbit circles so it can stay in familiar territory. When frightened, it often slips into a woodchuck burrow or brush pile.

You can often bag cottontails by walking through cover, looking for rabbits in their forms. Upland bird hunters flush rabbits by moving in typical walk-and-wait fashion. Like deer, a cottontail becomes nervous when a nearby hunter stands motionless and bounds from its resting spot.

Hunting with dogs offers an interesting and effective alternative. Most hunters use slow-moving hounds such as beagles and bassets. When the dogs get close, the cottontail begins moving in a large circle and eventually passes within shooting range of the hunter. Almost any dog will chase cottontails, but if it works too fast, the rabbit dashes under a brush pile or down a hole.

Rabbits may contract a bacterial disease called tularemia, which causes them to behave listlessly and eventually kills them. But the disease is rare. One researcher found it in only 2 of 12,000 rabbits he examined. Nevertheless, refrain from shooting rabbits that move slowly or otherwise behave unusually. Tularemia can be transmitted to humans who eat or handle the flesh of infected animals.

To hit zig-zagging cottontails, most hunters use shotguns with modified or improved cylinder chokes and No. 6 shot. But when rabbits are in their forms or feeding in the open, reach for a .22 rifle.

Cottontails are named for their fluffy white tail. The fur on the upper part of the body is grayish-brown with black tips. The undersides are white. Adults measure 14 to 19 inches (35.5 to 48.25 cm) long and weigh 2½ to 3½ pounds (1 to 1.5 kg).

WHERE TO FIND COTTONTAILS

Strip cover, like brushy fencelines and hedgerows, makes ideal cottontail habitat. The brush and high grass provide food and cover.

Abandoned farms offer a variety of hiding spots. Look for rabbits around groves, under old machinery or in tall grass or brush.

Brush piles provide good escape cover. A fox or owl would have little chance of reaching a rabbit beneath the logs and sticks.

Tracks of cottontails have side-by-side hind prints ahead of smaller front prints. One front foot falls ahead of the other.

Runways in tall grass serve as escape routes. Rabbits usually follow the same paths through cover, eventually matting down the vegetation.

Feeding signs include girdled shrubs or saplings and cleanly-snipped twigs. Cottontails prefer the bark of sumac and fruit trees.

HOW TO HUNT WITH HOUNDS

Release the dogs where you find plenty of sign. Beagles have excellent noses and scour the ground thoroughly to find fresh scent. They methodically follow the trail, slowly pushing the rabbit ahead.

Wait in the area where the dogs first detect fresh scent. A rabbit usually circles and returns to the spot where it was flushed. If it does not circle, try to predict its escape route, then attempt to intercept it.

Walk around the form in ever-widening circles. Look for the rabbit in clumps of brush, around the bases of trees, in tall grass or in any dense cover. Continue walking until you cover the entire area within a 100-foot (30 m) radius of the cottontail's form. Follow any fresh tracks you encounter.

Locate a form with fresh sign. Droppings are round and about ⅜ inch (95 mm) across. A rabbit seldom moves far from its form. Watch for rabbit tracks as you walk a strip of cover like a brushy fence line. A retriever or flushing dog will scare up tight-holding rabbits.

Hunt around abandoned farmsteads. Look for rabbits as you round the corner of a building and be ready for a quick shot. Flush cottontails by beating a brush pile with a stick. Or climb on top of the brush pile, jump up and down and yell to scare out rabbits.

JACKRABBIT

Black-tailed jackrabbits are found in low-lying semi-desert areas of the United States and Mexico. Jackrabbits (which are technically hares, not rabbits) may also be found in typical cottontail country and around tree plantations in more temperate climates. Night feeders, jackrabbits are best hunted in the low light of early morning and in the evening. Landowners are often happy to allow hunting to keep populations from destroying valuable alfalfa and other crops.

The black-tailed jackrabbit grows to a length of about 24 inches (60 cm) and adults weigh between 1 and 2 pounds (0.45 to 0.9 kg). They can reach speeds of up to 35 mph (55 km/h) and can leap up to 5 yards (6m) in a single jump.

One of the most productive methods for hunting jackrabbits is the drive. Groups of three to five hunters work the best. The hunters walk in a line through good rabbit habitat, spread out with about 10 yards (9 m) in between. The preferred tools are .22 rifles and 20-gauge shotguns. Rabbits will be pushed out ahead of the group or hold tight to run the opposite direction after the drive has moved past.

For safety's sake, high-visibility blaze orange is essential on these hunts and the group leader should ensure that the line stays intact.

When flushed, jackrabbits zig and zag, putting brush and distance between the hunter and hunted. Unlike cottontails, jackrabbits don't often circle back, they're headed for the horizon. Be ready, because you'll probably not get another chance.

Although blacktails are largely solitary animals, they may be found in large groups at certain times of the year, especially when feeding on a plot of alfalfa.

SNOWSHOE HARE

The snowshoe is named for its oversized hind feet, which provide a large surface area to support the animal on soft snow.

Snowshoes behave much like cottontails and eat similar foods. But they are more likely to feed at night. They prefer conifer swamps and young hardwood forests rather than brushy edges. Snowshoes are larger, faster and better jumpers.

A snowshoe can run up to 30 mph (48 km/h) and change direction in the middle of a leap, so a tight choke is less effective. To increase their shooting range, many still-hunters use .22 rifles.

Look for a snowshoe's black eye and black-tipped ears when hunting in snow. You can spot the animals more easily after a mid-winter thaw, because their white bodies stand out against bare ground.

Hunting with hounds works as well for snowshoes as it does for cottontails. Like cottontails, snowshoes will stay ahead of a dog and circle back toward a waiting hunter.

Snowshoes, also called varying hares, vary in color depending on the season. The coat is white in winter and brown in summer. Snowshoes are 16 to 21 inches (40.6 to 53.3 cm) long and weigh 3 to 4 pounds (1.3 to 1.8 kg).

Follow tracks after a fresh snowfall. About 2 inches (5 cm) of new snow over a hard crust makes for ideal tracking. If the snow is more than 1 foot (30 cm) deep, a pair of snowshoes make walking much easier.

GRAY SQUIRREL

Because the squirrel can provide a good meal for hawks, owls, weasels, minks, bobcats, foxes, coyotes or humans, he must be alert at all times—whether on the ground or high in a tree. A gray squirrel hunt is a test of marksmanship for any hunter. Using their wide-angle vision and sharp hearing, squirrels quickly detect danger.

To avoid being seen, a squirrel moves to the opposite side of a tree trunk or limb. Or it flattens its body against the tree. Once the hunter has walked past, it scampers to its den and stays there until it feels safe.

Good habitat produces one gray squirrel per acre (ha). Thus, 1 square mile (2.6 sq km) of prime woodlands could hold over 600 squirrels. How plentiful gray squirrels are in a given year depends mainly on the previous year's acorn crop. Other foods include walnuts, hickory nuts, pecans, berries and corn.

Gray squirrels begin feeding just before sunrise and they continue for two or three hours. They resume feeding in late afternoon and may remain active until after sunset. Squirrels move about most on calm, sunny days. Extreme cold or windy weather keeps them denned up. They seldom travel more than 300 yards (274 m) from their dens.

Mature deciduous forests throughout eastern North America hold gray squirrels. They favor mixed hardwoods with an abundance of mature oaks, dense undergrowth and few open areas.

Gray squirrels have a grayish back and sides and whitish or brownish undersides. A solid black color phase predominates in some areas. Adults measure 14 to 21 inches (35.5 to 53.3 cm) from head to tail and weigh ¾ to 1½ pounds (0.3 to 0.7 kg).

FOX SQUIRREL

Named for its reddish, fox-colored fur, the fox squirrel differs from the gray in behavior and habitat. Some hunters maintain that it is less wary and easier to outwit.

Fox squirrels spend more time on the ground than grays and rely less on treetops as escape routes. When threatened, they run straight for their dens or hide behind trunks or limbs. Unlike grays, they seldom feed in early morning. They are more active during midday and stray farther from their dens. Fox squirrels can often be seen lying on a limb basking in the sun.

Many hunters refer to fox squirrels as red squirrels. But the true red squirrel is much smaller and is not considered a game animal.

Fox squirrels prefer woodlots, farm groves and strips of timber rather than forests. Like grays, they eat acorns and other nuts. In agricultural areas, corn and other crops make up a high percentage of the diet. Squirrels get most of their water from their food.

Both gray and fox squirrels make a variety of calls. A series of rapid cherks or barks serves as a warning signal to other squirrels. The familiar chatter means squirrels are approaching one another. A low-pitched chuckle signifies contentment.

Adult fox squirrels measure 19 to 29 inches (48.25 to 73.75 cm) from head to tail and weigh 1 to 2¾ pounds (0.45 to 1.2 kg).

Hickory trees produce nuts that draw squirrels. You can easily identify hickories in early fall; they turn yellow earlier than other trees.

Acorn shells at the base of a tree indicate a squirrel den somewhere above. Sign in a large forest is usually left by grays.

Stripped corncobs also reveal squirrel activity. Sign along a fence line or in a small woodlot is generally that of fox squirrels.

Dens are made by squirrels gnawing at small openings like woodpecker holes. Dens are about 4 inches (10 cm) wide and at least 10 feet (3 m) off the ground.

Nests consist of twigs and leaves piled into a crotch or woven into the branches. Nests are 1 to 2 feet (30 to 60 cm) across and 20 feet (6 m) or more above ground.

Hunting for Squirrels

Look for stands of oak trees or other nut-producing trees. An old apple orchard close to timberlands may also produce good hunting.

Mast crops very from year to year and squirrels locate near this food. During late summer squirrels eat wild cherries, poplar buds, maple seeds, mulberries, gum berries and fruits, or the seeds of trees that ripen early.

As fall progresses squirrels start their heaviest feeding of the year, preparing for winter. They cut or feed on the nuts of pecan, hickory, walnut, oak or beech trees. Piles of small pieces of chewed nut hulls dropped on the ground under these trees, called cuttings, are evidence of feeding.

In agricultural areas, squirrels concentrate near cornfields; look for sign where squirrels have climbed cornstalks to eat the kernels off the cob or where they have pulled down the cobs.

During the warm days of early and mid-fall squirrels may start feeding at night and continue until after daylight, resting during the warm part of the day and feeding again in late evening. Feeding and storing nuts for winter lasts longer into the daylight hours as the season progresses. Later in the season squirrels spend more time on the ground gathering, digging and storing.

Hunting can be good during the squirrel's major breeding period, which starts in December or January. Squirrels lose their normal caution as they begin courtship, paying less attention to hunters.

The still-hunter watches for the slightest movement, the twitch of an ear, the flicker of a tail, the shine of an eye and listens for the cutting of teeth on nuts or the skittering of claws on bark. Freeze and investigate each noise. Windy or rainy weather covers your sound, allowing you to move through the woods with more stealth.

Stand-hunting can be the most productive tactic when the woods are too noisy to still-hunt. Sit quietly in a feeding area, watching for movement. Remain still after shooting one; sometimes squirrels resume normal activity after a few minutes.

Most squirrel hunters use .22 rifles with scopes up to 4×. Shotguns are a good choice; carry a .410 or a 20 or a 12-gauge with No. 6 shot.

Hiding on the opposite side of a tree trunk is the squirrel's favorite method of eluding the hunter. No matter where the hunter is, the squirrel is always on the other side of the tree.

HOW TO STAND-HUNT FOR SQUIRRELS

Sit quietly, glassing trees with binoculars. Choose a spot with the sun at your back. That way, you can see squirrels but they may not see you.

Call to coax squirrels into revealing themselves. Calls include a blow call (left) and a bellows call (right). Either can be used to produce barks and chatters.

Click coins together to imitate a scolding squirrel. Place one coin slightly lower than the other and rapidly snap the lower coin.

OTHER SQUIRREL HUNTING TECHNIQUES

Team-hunt with a companion. With this method, squirrels cannot hide on the opposite side of a tree without being seen. Be ready to shoot the moment a squirrel moves to your side of the tree.

Toss a stick or rock to the opposite side of a tree. Or tie a string to a bush on one side of the tree, then move to the other side and tug it sharply. The motion will frighten squirrels to your side.

Float-hunt along streams bordered by nut trees. The extra sunlight and moisture result in good nut crops that attract squirrels.

PRAIRIE DOG

The prairie dog is a creature of the western plains, found in the United States, Canada and Mexico. It grows to a length of 12 to 16 inches (30 to 40 cm). Prairie dogs live in large colonies or dog towns that can cover hundreds of acres (ha) of land.

They live in groups that consist of one male and two to four females. Females have one litter a year and give birth to an average of three or four pups. Prairie dogs feed on grass, insects and broadleaf plants. A great tunneler, this creature may dig 15 feet (4.5 m) downward and 100 feet (30 m) in a lateral direction. A tunnel system generally has several escape tunnels. The prairie dog has color vision and can detect danger at a great distance. To warn each other, prairie dogs use vocalizations.

Hunters can use rimfire rifles, but most hunters find that a center-fire rifle is a better choice to make shots on animals out to 400 yards (366 m). The 204 Ruger, 223 Remington and 22-250 Remington, stoked with thin-jacketed bullets are great options for prairie dog hunting.

A variable rifle scope is a big help out on the fields. And a bipod or shooting sticks can make the difference when every little bit of accuracy counts. Often the quarry is almost hidden behind a mound of dirt, leaving you a target no bigger than a silver dollar.

Prairie dogs may emerge from their dens during late winter warming trends, and are quite visible against the snow. Prairie dogs have dichromatic color vision, which allows them to detect predators over a long distance. A system of vocal communication enables them to quickly spread the alarm.

Herbivorous, the prairie dog thrives on a diet of grasses and broadleaf plants. Grasses are trimmed around the colony to remove cover that might hide a coyote, fox, or ferret.

GROUND SQUIRREL

Without food cultivated by humans, ground squirrels do not often grow out of balance. They live in small groups and are kept in check by birds of prey and sharp-toothed predators. But give a rodent an alfalfa field and everything changes. Before long, food becomes so plentiful that they don't have anything left to work at except procreation. Soon there are more ground squirrels than a rancher can feed.

Ground squirrels are members of the family Sciuridae, of the Marmotini tribe. Several different types of ground squirrels can be found. In some cases, the ground squirrel is found in small numbers and can be still-hunted. In cultivated fields, a hunter might spend all day in one place, shooting from an elevated stand.

As a team, two hunters can take turns spotting and shooting. Binoculars can help the spotter direct the shots. Such work makes both hunters more proficient. For the young shooter, looking forward to his or her first big game season, the practice is invaluable. April and May are the prime months for shooting as crops sprout and grow through last year's stubble. By mid-June, the grass may be too tall for spotting.

Property owners are often happy to let you shoot, but permission must be obtained. Keep in mind that well-traveled highways carry the most hunters and access might be easier to find off the beaten path. Establish relationships with landowners prior to the hunt or contact an outfitter for a guided shoot on private land.

For years, hunters have used rimfire .22s to good effect, but today there are better choices. The .22s, except in the most practiced hands, are rarely accurate past 100 yards (91 m).

An alternative is one of the 17 caliber rimfires. Based on the .22 Long Rifle or the .22 Magnum case, the 17-caliber bullet tips the scale at half the weight of the .22 projectile and can be accurate to 200 yards (183 m).

Abundant ground squirrel populations offer hunters the chance to improve long-range shooting skills. Over the course of a long day in the field, a marksman may fire 500 rounds or more.

RACCOON

Equipped with needle-sharp teeth and a quick temper, the raccoon is a fighter and a challenge to the houndsman/hunter. They may run for miles (km) and when cornered, can kill or maim hunting dogs twice their size.

Hardwood forests near water make good raccoon habitat. They also live in marshy lowlands and can adapt to habitats ranging from the Florida mangroves to the arid plains of New Mexico.

Raccoon eat almost any kind of food including berries, fruits, nuts, frogs, crayfish and insects. Sweet corn is a favorite. They hold their food with small, nimble paws.

An adult raccoon may travel up to 5 miles (8 km) on its nightly feeding rounds, especially in warm weather. During the day they often den up in hollow trees. But they may bed in the tall vegetation along the edge of a marsh, in a culvert or in the ground burrow of another animal. Raccoon frequently use different dens or beds on successive days. They den up for a period after heavy snow; in cold climates they may hibernate.

Ranked among the most intelligent game animals, raccoon also have excellent hearing and good eyesight.

Raccoon have a black, mask-like band across the eyes and black rings on the tail. Most raccoon weigh between 15 and 20 pounds (6.75 and 9 kg). The largest on record, 62 pounds, 6 ounces, (28.1 kg) was shot in Wisconsin in 1950.

They can run up to 15 mph (24 km/h) and are good swimmers.

The vast majority of raccoon hunting is done with hounds, especially Walkers, black-and-tans and redbones. Tracking is easiest on damp, cool nights with a slight breeze. Some dogs can pick up a cold trail, making it possible to hunt in daylight.

When pursued by hounds, raccoon usually run in large circles, crawling in and out of holes and climbing up and down trees to lose the dogs. They may jump

to the ground from as high as 50 feet (15 m) and scurry away unharmed. They stay in a tree only when the hounds get so close that other avenues of escape are impossible.

Early in the season you may be able to call raccoon. After dark, take a stand along a stream bank, lakeshore or cornfield. Use calls to imitate an injured bird or rabbit.

Most raccoon hunters use .22 rifles, although some prefer 20-gauge shotguns with No. 6 or 7½ shot. Where legal, a few hunters use small-caliber handguns.

WHERE TO FIND RACCOON

Look for holes in trees that could be den sites (left). You seldom see raccoon during the day, but an area with many dens would be a good spot to hunt after dark.

Check for tracks in the soft dirt around ponds, marshes or streams. Raccoon go to water to drink and to find foods like crayfish, frogs and small fish.

HOW TO HUNT WITH HOUNDS

Release the hounds and allow them to range ahead to pick up raccoon scent. To better control the hounds, some hunters keep them on leash until the dogs detect fresh scent, then turn them loose (left).

Listen for the hounds to start baying, then follow the sound. Some hunters use orange or red headlamps to find their way through the woods. The colored light is less noticeable to a raccoon than a white light.

Continue to follow the dogs until they either tree the raccoon or lose it. Sometimes the chase goes on for miles (km). Hunters can tell when their dogs tree a raccoon, because the baying becomes more intense.

COYOTE

The coyote, once an inhabitant of the Western plains, has spread across the continent. They are thriving now because of humans. In the late-1800s and early-1900s, ranchers and trappers declared war on wolves. For decades, the coyote's ancient enemy has been largely absent from the lower 48 states. With little competition, coyotes have taken over. And, they have become educated about how to live around people. Even within the city limits of big cities, coyotes prowl golf courses and fields in search of their prey. In the suburbs, residents complain about the coyotes that roam at will, eating from dog food dishes and garbage cans or picking up unsuspecting dogs and cats.

A good place to hunt coyotes is wherever they can find their principal foods. Fields, meadows and prairies are full of mice; brushy draws hold rabbits and upland birds. Wherever there are antelope or deer, there will be coyotes close by. In the spring when ungulates are giving birth to their young, a fawn-in-distress call can draw in predators.

When you find an area that has all the right coyote foods, look for sign. Coyotes use trails and waterholes just like the other animals. If there are coyotes in the area, you'll soon see their sign.

An adult coyote stands less than 24 inches (61 cm) tall and varies in color from whitish-gray to brown with sometimes a reddish cast to its pelt. Ears and nose appear long and pointed, in relation to the size of its head. It weighs between 20 and 50 pounds (9 and 22.5 kg) and can be identified by a thick, bushy tail, which it often holds low to the ground. He is an extremely lean, fast animal that may reach speeds up to 43 mph (69 km/h).

Coyote droppings are about the same size as a dog's of similar size but the scat is small and twisted on the end. It contains undigested bits of whatever the animal has been feeding on. Deer hair, bits of rabbit and mouse fur and even berries are found in coyote droppings.

Coyotes also need a den to raise their pups in spring and summer and for shelter in extreme conditions. A good coyote hunting area will be adjacent to food sources but also give ample cover to hide from their enemies.

In September and October the young of the year are out searching for food on their own. The population is strongest at this time of the year and many coyotes are taken during deer and elk seasons. But the coyote pelt is best after the first snows and a tanned pelt or a coyote rug makes a fine trophy to remember a successful hunt.

Calling Coyotes

A fawn-in-distress or a dying rabbit predator call costs only a few dollars and can be easily mastered. Electronic calls with remote controls and motorized decoys cost more, but provide a way for the hunter to watch the call from a distance.

The first two hours and last two hours of daylight are the best times for calling. A coyote may respond anytime of day but the likelihood is greater at first and last light.

The coyote knows that the sound of a rabbit or a rodent in distress means an easy meal, if it can take the prey away from whatever is killing it. That is why sometimes a dominant coyote comes right in while a younger dog might be hesitant.

Put fright and pain in the calling. The first sounds a rabbit makes when it is captured are a series of squalls

Coyotes normally have a territory of 10 to 40 square miles (26 to 104 sq km). They can sprint up to 35 mph (56 km/h), fast enough to overtake a deer. A coyote's track looks similar to that of a domestic dog.

which then become gasping cries. If the predator shifts its grip then the squalls might come again.

Study the land and determine likely approaches a coyote might make. The wind is of paramount importance. Situate yourself downwind from where the coyote is likely to be. Situate hunting partners up to 50 yards (45 m) away from the caller.

Wear full camouflage and grease paint on hands and face. Keep all movement to a minimum. As coyotes approach they zero-in on the location of the caller.

Call in one location for at least 20 minutes.

Depending on the topography you might need only move a quarter of a mile before calling again.

For a dedicated coyote rifle, the best choice might be one of the flat-shooting .22 center-fires or a 6mm or .243. Beyond these, any rifle a big-game hunter is proficient with is the perfect choice for coyotes.

For calling situations where the coyote is likely to come in close, a shotgun is ideal. Use a load with sufficient knockdown power in the range between No. 2 and 00 buckshot.

Coyotes perform a valuable function, keeping rodent and rabbit populations in check. However, as coyote populations increase they can put a severe dent in the numbers of deer and antelope herds.

Coyotes are on the move when snow is on the ground. The cold weather speeds up metabolisms, making them vulnerable to the sound of a prey animal in distress.

A shot at a coyote might be taken as close as 10 feet (3 m) or as far out as 300 yards (274 m). A good coyote gun should be able to accommodate either circumstance.

Some callers use confidence decoys to lure the coyotes in. Jackrabbit, cottontail and fawn decoys give the coyote something to look at as it approaches. Other hunters simply use an old stuffed animal that approximates the natural.

Chapter 6

HUNTING UPLAND GAME BIRDS

The memories that are made in the fall are the kind of images that stay with you for the rest of your life.

Dried stalks of corn rattling with the November breeze and the sudden rush of wings that is a gaudy ringneck rooster clawing for altitude. Chukar running the ridge top in front of a flushing dog, then a dozen birds briefly silhouetted against the sky. A German shorthair quivering on point, his eyes locked on a patch of color in the grass. The heft and grace of a fine double gun coming to your shoulder.

Upland bird hunting is a multi-faceted sport. Bird hunters cherish guns that they shoot well and spend months training their dogs for a few days afield each year. Some hunters focus on one or two species, but the continent holds a variety of game bird opportunities, from farmland pheasants to mountain quail, to the challenge of chukar.

Upland gunning is sport for hunters of any economic background and experience. Upland bird hunts are the province of anyone with a shotgun and a license, whether a nine-year-old novice or a well-traveled sportsman.

The term upland means high ground. But upland birds can also be found in and around lowlands. Pheasants frequent marsh edges and sharp-tailed grouse often live in bogs. Migratory upland birds also congregate in lowland areas. Woodcock feed along moist stream banks and mourning doves gather near water holes.

Upland bird hunters need little equipment other than waterproof boots and a thorn-proof jacket and pants. With the exception of the small-caliber rifles used for wild turkey, upland bird hunters almost always use shotguns. The choke and shot size varies with the size of the bird and the usual shooting distance.

RING-NECKED PHEASANT

Imported from Asia in the 1880s, the pheasant fast became a favorite. The bird is a walking, flying kaleidoscope of color. Flashing blue, purple, copper and iridescent green, it rises out of the amber grain in a blur of wings and sound.

The pheasant deserves its reputation as one of the most wily and elusive upland game birds. Its first instinct is to run rather than fly. And despite its large size and gaudy colors, a rooster can slink away unnoticed in ankle-high cover. Sometimes a bird sits tight, refusing to budge unless you actually step on it.

Pheasants rely on excellent eyesight and good hearing to elude hunters. They can detect ground vibrations not recognizable to humans. These vibrations often cause roosters to crow.

Ringnecks thrive in fertile agricultural areas with good nesting and wintering cover. In spring, they nest in moderately dense cover like hay meadows, clover fields and roadside ditches. They continue to use these areas as roosting sites into the fall, but also roost in weedy crop fields, short slough grass, willow patches and woodlots. They occasionally roost in trees. Pheasants need heavier cover to escape winter storms.

Primary foods include grain crops like corn, wheat, milo and soybeans. They also eat weed seeds and insects. The birds pick up grit in fields and along roads. This helps their gizzard to grind food.

From June through August, hen pheasants remain with their broods of four to eight chicks. By fall, the chicks begin to mature and the groups break up. As winter approaches, pheasants often flock together where they can find food and heavy cover. Flocks may contain hundreds of birds.

Despite the fact that pheasants are among the hardiest of game birds, their average life-span is only nine months. Normally, only 30 percent of the birds survive from one year to the next, even where there is no hunting season.

In most states and provinces, only roosters are legal game. Pheasant roosters can mate with many hens. Research has proven that hunters can harvest up to 90 percent of the roosters without affecting the next year's hatch.

Hunters can quickly distinguish the colorful rooster from the drab hen. In addition, roosters often cackle on take-off, removing any doubt about the bird's sex. The typical rooster measures 30 to 36 inches (76 to 91 cm) from head to tail and weighs 2½ to 3 pounds (1 to 1.3 kg). The hen has a much shorter tail and weighs about ½ pound less (0.25 kg).

Roosters have spurs on the lower part of the leg. The spurs grow longer and sharper as the bird gets older, reaching ¾-inch (1.9 cm) on three-year-old birds. They use their spurs in spring territorial battles. The sharp spurs on an old rooster can badly scratch a hunter or a dog.

When a rooster bursts from cover, it quickly reaches a speed of 35 to 40 mph (56 to 64 km/h). It may fly up to 1 mile (1.6 km), but usually only a few hundred yards (m). A bird generally spends its entire life in an area of ½ square mile (1.3 sq km) or less, leaving that area only if food or cover becomes inadequate.

Hunting pheasant is most glorious for what returns in memories. Good friends, a hard-working dog, long-tailed birds and sunlight on steel barrels.

WHERE TO FIND PHEASANTS

Wild ringnecks are often found in wheat, corn, barley and milo fields, feeding on grain, weed seeds and insects. Thick, brushy cover along fence rows, ditches, streams and marshes provide cover.

Pheasants feed in the morning and evening, then retreat to rest. Ideal habitat includes water, cover and feed within a short walk. Early morning and evening are good times to listen for calling.

When working brushy fence rows, one or two drivers should bust through the weeds with a dog, searching a ragged pattern back and forth. Post another hunter at the end of the row to jump skulking birds into the air. Expect pressured pheasants to seek out steep, brushy draws that defy all but the most determined.

Ringnecks get their name from the white ring around the rooster's neck. Both sexes have brownish tails with black crossbars. The rooster has a reddish-copper breast and a powder-blue rump. Its head has shades of metallic blue, green and purple with a bright red eye patch.

The hen is tan with dark flecks and creamy mottling.

TYPICAL PHEASANT HABITAT

Nesting cover is vital to pheasants (left). Hens need grassy cover at least 12 inches (30 cm) high which remains unmowed until after nesting.

Fertile croplands offer a good food supply. But expanses of corn and other row crops with little cover support few pheasants.

Winter cover includes cattail sloughs, thick brush or willows and woodlots. With good cover, pheasants can survive to −50°F (−45°C).

When hunting in standing corn, post blockers at the end of the rows to jump roosters into the air. Avoid shooting at birds until they are above the stalks to avoid endangering other hunters.

Pheasant Hunting Strategies

The pheasant hunting season can be split into two parts: the first few days and the rest of the season. Young pheasants lack the wariness of birds hatched the previous year, so the early days of the season usually offer the easiest hunting. Once the easier birds are gone, you will find it much more difficult to outwit the remaining roosters.

EARLY SEASON. You can locate a good area before the season opens by driving through the countryside and looking for pheasants. The best time to spot the birds is around sunrise on a clear, calm day with dew on the grass. You may also see pheasants in late afternoon. Another way to locate a good hunting area is to look for abundant nesting cover. Chances are there are birds in the vicinity. If you find a promising location, ask the farmer if you can return to hunt once the season begins.

Early-season hunters often find most of the land covered with crops. In this situation, pheasants may be almost anywhere. To flush birds from large crop or stubble fields, hunters conduct drives. With this much cover still standing, other techniques may not be as productive.

Ringnecks usually flush close in early season, so a shotgun with an improved cylinder or modified choke works best. Use shot no larger than No. 6.

LATE SEASON. Once farmers harvest their crops, the birds have fewer places to hide. But birds that survive to late season have learned to evade danger and often flush far ahead of approaching hunters. Or they hold extremely tight and let hunters walk past.

In late season, roosters hole up in much heavier cover than they did earlier in the year. They prefer areas with tall trees or other cover that breaks the wind. Look for them in brushy woodlots, thick fence lines and drainage ditches lined with slough grass. A favorite hiding spot is a fringe of cattails around the edge of a shallow wetland. Although it prefers heavy cover, a late-season rooster sometimes seeks refuge in a patch of grass not much larger than his body. After a snowfall, hunters often find pheasants under clumps of grass covered with snow. The birds evidently allow themselves to become snowed in.

To bag late-season roosters, one hunter blocks a possible escape route while another approaches from the opposite end of cover. If a rooster flushes too far ahead of the walking hunter, the blocker may get a shot.

For long-range shooting in late season, use a modified or full choke shotgun with No. 4 to 6 shot.

Hunting Pheasants with a Dog

Statistics show that hunters who use dogs bag twice as many ringnecks as those who do not. Most hunters agree that flushers and retrievers work best in heavy cover. Preferred breeds include springer spaniels and Labrador retrievers. Some hunters prefer pointing dogs for large expanses of light, grassy cover, but a wily rooster often runs rather than hold to a point.

A dog with good retrieving skills seldom loses a crippled ringneck. Pheasants are notoriously difficult to kill. A wounded rooster usually runs off and burrows under heavy grass or brush, where a hunter without a dog would have practically no chance of finding it. A good dog marks the bird down and relentlessly pursues it through even the thickest tangle of vegetation.

Skilled handlers refuse to work their dogs in standing cornfields or fields of other tall row crops. To a ringneck, an open row is an invitation to run. And most dogs follow, often disappearing into the field and flushing birds at the opposite end.

A novice pheasant hunter tends to over-command his dog, continually directing it to hunt likely-looking spots. Instead, let the dog use its nose to decide where to hunt. Allow it to range back and forth across cover until it finds fresh scent.

Hunt strip cover with your dog on the downwind side. When the dog detects fresh scent, it moves into the cover and flushes or points the bird. Late in the season, another hunter should post at the end of the strip.

Follow your dog through a large expanse of cover. A flushing dog may run when it picks up a scent. You must keep up so birds do not flush out of range. With pointing breeds, you do not have to stay as close.

Send your dog into a thick patch of cover to save you time and energy. Keep track of its location by watching and listening for moving grass or brush. Or, attach a bell to the dog's collar.

General Tactics

A ringneck's inclination to run rather than fly makes it one of the most difficult birds to hunt by yourself. But you can greatly improve your odds by choosing the right type of spot and by using proven techniques.

You are most likely to flush pheasants from small, isolated pieces of cover, such as a patch of short slough grass surrounded by a plowed field. In a large block of heavy cover, a rooster can easily give you the slip.

If you walk steadily in a straight line, pheasants probably sit tight and let you pass. But if you follow a zig-zag path, walking a few steps, then stopping for a moment, nearby pheasants generally become nervous and fly.

Watch and listen carefully for any indication of pheasant movement. If the cover is not too thick, you might catch a glimpse of a rooster running ahead. On a still day, you may hear the slight rustling of a rooster sneaking through the grass.

Driving for Pheasants

Driving takes advantage of the ringneck's habit of running at the sight or sound of humans. A row of hunters moves through all or part of a large block of cover, while posters wait quietly at the end.

Drivers may flush some pheasants, but more often the birds run to the end of the field. When the drivers approach the posters, the birds realize they are trapped and explode from cover.

TIPS FOR HUNTING PHEASANTS

Select manageable-sized pieces of cover. Try to push the birds toward a spot where the cover suddenly ends. Pheasants are reluctant to run into an open field and usually flush near the edge.

Look for the tallest, thickest cover, especially in cold or windy weather. Trees or tall weeds offer better shelter than the surrounding lower cover.

Hunt the sunny side of cover on frosty mornings. Pheasants move to the sunlit side to warm up and dry ant moisture on their feathers. Later in the day, the birds may retreat deeper into the cover.

Follow fresh tracks in the snow. Rooster tracks are slightly larger and farther apart than those of a hen. Often the tracks end at a snow-covered clump of grass. You may have to kick the clump to flush the bird.

Drive pheasants from the heaviest cover to the lightest. Pushing birds into sparse vegetation forces them to fly. If you drive from light to heavy cover, the birds are more likely to find a safe hiding spot.

Avoid driving into the sun, especially when it is low in the sky. The glare may blind you or prevent you from distinguishing a rooster from a hen. If you must hunt into the sun, listen for a cackle or look for a long tail.

Leapfrog stretches of cover. Drop off a partner, drive ahead, then start walking. He or she walks to the car, drives ahead of you, then resumes walking.

Choose dirty crop fields when hunting ringnecks. The weeds provide cover and food that is lacking in clean, well-manicured fields. Look for the tallest, thickest habitat, especially in cold or windy weather. Trees or tall weeds offer better shelter than the surrounding lower cover.

If the field is too wide to cover in one pass, the posters can take a vehicle to the end they are blocking. The drivers can take the vehicle back to the opposite end, then make another drive. Or the posters can return, while the drivers start another pass from the end where they finished.

When driving cover that narrows toward one end, start from the widest end. This way you will push the birds into a smaller area, increasing the likelihood of someone getting a shot.

BOBWHITE QUAIL

A covey of bobwhites exploding from cover can rattle even the veteran hunter. Often, each bird flies in a different direction. In the confusion, you may shoot hurriedly without touching a feather.

Despite their stubby wings, quail can fly up to 30 mph (48 km/h) and change direction instantly as they dodge through cover. But they usually fly less than 200 yards (183 m). Bobwhites are also excellent runners; in fact, they seldom fly unless threatened.

When alarmed, a member of the covey emits a barely audible signal which tells the others to freeze. They squat and remain motionless, relying on camouflage for concealment until the threat passes. If they feel too conspicuous, they scurry to another hiding spot.

Cocks have a white throat patch and a white line through the eye. On hens, the throat patch and line are buff-colored. Bobwhites measure about 10 inches (25 cm) long and weigh 6 to 8 ounces (170 to 226 g).

Unlike pheasants, bobwhites are monogamous, meaning that a cock breeds with only one hen. Quail eggs hatch from May to early July. The cock helps incubate the eggs and raise the chicks. By the start of

Bobwhite quail roost on the ground. During cool weather, they form a roosting ring, huddling in a plate-sized circle with their tails pointing toward the center. This tactic preserves body heat. Bobwhites prefer a roosting site with plenty of open space above them, enabling them to flush quickly should the need arise. Roosts generally have a south or west exposure, so the ground stays warm in late afternoon.

hunting season, the chicks resemble the adults and the covey consists of 10 to 15 birds.

The birds thrive in areas with a mixture of grasslands, woodlands and brush adjacent to croplands. They use grasslands mainly for nesting; woodlands and brush provide roosting and escape cover. Bobwhites cannot survive in a climate with prolonged periods of deep snow or severe cold. They are unable to dig through deep snow to find food and their small bodies do not retain enough heat.

Nearly all bobwhites live within 50 to 100 feet (15 to 30 m) of field borders. They are seldom found in the middle of a crop field or woods.

The bobwhite's diet consists mainly of weed seeds, but they also eat insects, acorns and crops like corn, soybeans, wheat and milo. On hot, clear days, the birds feed in early morning and late afternoon. In midday, they take periodic dust baths along sunny field edges. But during cool, damp weather, bobwhites often stay in their roosts until mid-morning, feed intermittently until dark, then return to their roosts.

Each year, predators, severe weather and hunting take a heavy toll on the bobwhite population. On the average, a bird lives about 8½ months; only 15 to 20 percent survive to the next breeding season.

Hunting for Bobwhite Quail

To many bobwhite hunters, the biggest thrill comes from watching good pointing dogs in action.

A lone hunter who works the cover slowly and thoroughly can kick up some bobwhites by himself. But if the birds decide to hold tight, hunting can be extremely difficult without a dog.

Most hunters prefer English pointers or English setters for large expanses of cover. Brittanys and German shorthairs also work well, but do not cover quite as much ground. Handlers allow the dogs to range far ahead of the hunting party. When a dog detects fresh scent, it locks on point. The covey freezes, giving the hunters plenty of time to move into position.

Most of the birds burst from cover in unison. After the initial flush, work the area a little longer because a straggler or two may remain. Flushing the last birds is often more difficult.

Quail usually fly only a short distance, so you can flush them again. Sometimes the covey stays together, sometimes it breaks up. Watch carefully because the birds may veer off to the side just before they land.

Early season offers the best bobwhite hunting. Coveys consist mainly of young birds that have never been hunted. But as the season progresses, quail become much more unpredictable. Some birds flush when you slam your car door. Others run rather than hold. Flushed birds fly two or three times farther than they did in early season.

Finding downed quail can be difficult, even with a good dog. Some hunters maintain that the scent washes off as the birds fly. On the ground, bobwhites compress their feathers so little scent can escape. Bird dogs may walk within inches (cm) of wounded quail without finding them. Because of their small size and excellent camouflage, quail can hide in the lightest cover. Wear snakeproof chaps or leggings to protect yourself from snakebites. They also protect your legs from tough thorns and briers.

Many quail hunters prefer 20-gauge, double-barreled shotguns with improved cylinder and modified chokes. Small shot, usually No. 7½ or 8, works best.

WHERE TO FIND BOBWHITE QUAIL

Osage orange means good quail cover. Its sharp spines prevent cattle from eating the underbrush. Look for the large, yellow fruits.

Giant ragweed provides roosting and escape cover. The plants stand up to 12 feet (3.6 m) tall. Ragweed seeds may be a major source of food in fall.

Lespedeza or Japan Clover, produces seeds which quail eat in winter. Found mainly in the southern United States, it is planted for erosion control.

Pick a single bird and concentrate on that shot. Resist the tendency to flock shoot. A wild shot at the covey rarely brings down a bird.

Learn to judge your effective shooting distance. Because bobwhites are so small, they are probably closer than you think.

Wear snakeproof chaps or leggings to protect yourself from snakebites. They also protect from tough thorns and briers.

Listen for the typical bob-bob-white whistle during the mating period. You will find birds in the same area once the hunting season opens.

CALIFORNIA QUAIL

California quail are also called valley quail. They prefer semi-arid desert brushlands. They feed on the seeds of weeds and brush and roost in dense patches of tall shrubs or low trees. The birds need water each day and are seldom far from streams, springs or water holes.

In fall, they form large flocks numbering from 50 to over 100 birds. They prefer to run rather than fly. When flushed, they usually go only a short distance, then land in bushes or trees.

A good pointing dog can pin down an entire covey by circling the birds. If they fly, watch where they land. They hold tighter on the second flush.

Ideal shotguns for California quail are 12- or 20-gauge double barrels with modified and improved cylinder chokes. These guns give you an open pattern for birds that hold and a tight pattern for those that flush at long range. Most hunters use No. 7½ shot.

California quail, also called valley quail, can be found up and down the West Coast of North America, from southern British Columbia to the tip of the Baja Peninsula. They are a ground-dwelling and foraging bird that seldom moves far from the place where they were hatched. The coveys feed on seasonal seeds, leaves, and insects and search out sunny spots to take communal dust baths.

In fall, they form large packs numbering from 50 to over 100 birds. They prefer to run rather than fly. When flushed, they are loud flyers, bursting like popcorn from cover. They scatter to confuse predators and seldom fly very far, landing in bushes and trees.

These quail are native to the Southwest, but they have been introduced to other places around the world, including Australia, New Zealand, and Hawaii.

California quail prefer semi-arid desert brushlands. They feed on the seeds of weeds and brush, and roost in dense patches of tall shrubs or low trees. The birds need water each day and are seldom far from streams, springs, or water holes.

A good pointing dog can pin down an entire covey by circling the birds. If they fly, watch where they land. They hold tighter on the second flush.

Ideal shotguns for the quail on these pages are 12- or 20-gauge double barrels with modified and improved cylinder chokes. These guns give you an open pattern for birds that hold and a tight pattern for those that flush at long range. Most hunters use No. 7½ shot.

California quail have a scaled breast, grayish brown flanks with white streaks and a teardrop-shaped plume. Males have a black throat with a white border and a chestnut patch on the belly. Females are less boldly marked. California quail weigh 6 to 7 ounces (170 to 198 g).

GAMBEL'S QUAIL

Sometimes called desert quail, Gambel's quail are usually found along brushy slopes and in river valleys of arid and semi-arid deserts. They roost in dense thickets or trees and feed on the seeds of weeds and brush. Normally the birds get enough water from their foods and the dew. But during dry conditions, they rely on a watering site.

The birds come out to feed early and late. They spend the rest of the day in brushy cover to escape the heat. In cool weather, they leave their roosts earlier and may remain in the open all day.

If you approach Gambel's quail in the open, they will probably run before you can get a shot. But if you wait until they move to cover, the birds are more likely to hold. A good pointing dog improves your odds.

Poisonous snakes are rarely a problem, but some hunters wear leather or plastic leggings.

The Gambel's quail was named after William Gambel, a 19th century explorer of the southwestern United States. Sometimes called desert quail, Gambel's quail inhabit the southwestern desert country of California, Arizona, Colorado, New Mexico, Nevada, Texas, Utah, and Sonora, Mexico. Non-migratory,

they are usually found along brushy slopes and in river valleys of arid and semi-arid deserts. They roost in dense thickets or trees, and feed on the seeds of weeds and brush. Normally the birds get enough water from their foods and the dew. But during dry conditions, they rely on a watering site.

The Gambel's average length is 11 inches (30 cm). It has a wingspan of 14 to 16 inches (35 to 40 cm). It moves through cover by walking and when pushed can run surprisingly fast. Its flight, like that of its cousin the California quail, is abrupt, explosive, and terminated by a long glide to the ground.

The birds come out to feed early and late. They spend the rest of the day in brushy cover to escape the heat. In cool weather, they leave their roosts earlier and may remain in the open all day.

If you approach Gambel's quail in the open, they will probably run before you can get a shot. But if you wait until they move to cover, the birds are more likely to hold. A good pointing dog will improve your odds.

In the cooler weather of hunting season, poisonous snakes are rarely a problem, but some hunters wear leather or plastic leggings.

Gambel's quail resemble California quail, but their buff-white belly is not scaled and the cap and flanks on the male are reddish brown. Males also have a black patch on the lower part of the breast. Gambel's quail weigh 5½ to 6½ ounces (156 to 184 g).

MOUNTAIN QUAIL

Few upland game birds are as difficult to hunt as mountain quail. They run at the sight of a hunter and even a good pointing dog has difficulty pinning them down. A flusher or retriever is more likely to find single birds that sit tight.

Found at elevations of 2,000 to 10,000 feet (610 to 3,048 m), mountain quail live along brushy edges of conifer forests and streams. They eat berries, clover, wild oats and seeds of weeds and grasses; the birds roost under heavy brush or in small trees. Home territories take in large areas. They head to lower elevations in late fall to avoid severe weather.

Coveys generally number only seven to nine birds. They do not form large coveys, but hunters sometimes see loose groups of birds feeding in the same area.

Listen for the call any time of day, but pay close attention in the evening, as feeding birds reassemble near water prior to roosting. Food and cover are the keys to finding quail and to the lasting memory of a full game bag at the end of the day.

Few upland game birds are as difficult to hunt as mountain quail. They will run at the sight of a hunter, and even a good pointing dog has difficulty pinning them down.

Found at elevations of 2,000 to 10,000 feet (610 to 3048 m), the mountain quail inhabits mountainous chaparral in California, Oregon, and Washington. They live along brushy edges of conifer forests and streams. Mountain quail eat berries, clover, wild oats, and seeds of weeds and grasses; the birds roost under heavy brush or in small trees. They are not migratory, but their home territories take in large areas. They seek out seasonally available foods and head to lower elevations in late fall to avoid severe weather.

Like other quail, they move about primarily by walking. When they run, they can cover ground at an amazing rate of speed. When startled, they run through cover and flush when they hit an opening. The birds scatter when they fly then regroup by calling.

Coveys generally number only seven to nine birds. They do not form large coveys, but hunters sometimes see loose groups of birds feeding in the same area.

A flusher or retriever is more likely to find single birds that sit tight.

Listen for the call any time of day, but pay close attention in the evening, as feeding birds reassemble near water prior to roosting. Food and cover are the keys to quail, and to the lasting memory of a full game bag at the end of the day.

Mountain quail have a grayish-brown back, a chestnut throat and chestnut flank with heavy white bars. The head and breast are bluish-gray. Two long, dark feathers form the plume. The sexes look alike. Mountain quail weigh 8 to 9 ounces (227 to 255 g).

SCALED QUAIL

Some hunters refer to scaled quail as blue quail; others call them cottontops or blue racers. These birds are even more likely to run than mountain quail.

Scaled quail live in semi-arid desert grasslands and in grassy brushlands. They prefer weed and brush seeds for food. The birds roost in dense clumps of brush, grass or weeds. Their water requirements are similar to those of Gambel's quail. In some states and provinces, conservation agencies have installed watering devices, helping both quail species to survive during dry periods.

Scaled quail country can be hard on the dog. Snakes are a concern, but the most important thing is to carry enough water for both hunter and dog. Lava rock and cactus play havoc with a dog's paws. Bring boots and ointment to protect Fido's feet.

If you spot a covey, rush the birds to startle them into flying. Even if you are out of range, shoot to scatter the birds and scare up stragglers. Then hunt the singles, because they are more likely to hold.

Some hunters refer to scaled quail as blue quail; others call them cottontops or blue racers. They are named for their scaly appearance on back and breast feathers. They can be identified by their cotton-like white crest.

They are bluish-gray birds that live in semi-arid desert grasslands and in grassy brushlands. The scaled quail and its subspecies are found in parts of Colorado, New Mexico, Arizona, western Oklahoma, and Texas, as well as Sonora and Chihuahua in Mexico. The chestnut-bellied scaled quail is found in southern Texas down to northwestern Mexico.

They prefer weed and brush seeds for food. The birds roost in dense clumps of brush, grass, or weeds. Their water requirements are similar to those of Gambel's quail. In some states conservation agencies have installed watering devices, helping both quail species to survive during dry periods.

Scaled quail country can be hard on dogs. Snakes are a concern, but the cooler weather of hunting season is likely to keep them dormant. The most important thing is to carry enough water for both hunter and dog. Lava rock and cactus play havoc with a dog's paws. Bring boots and ointment to protect Fido's feet.

These birds are even more likely to run than mountain quail. If you spot a covey, rush the birds to startle them into flying. Even if you are out of range, shoot to scatter the birds and scare up stragglers. Then hunt the singles, because they will be more likely to hold.

Scaled quail have breast feathers with dark margins, giving them a scaled appearance. The breast is bluish-gray; the head grayish-brown with a distinctive white-tipped crest. The crest is larger on males. Scaled quail weigh 6 to 7 ounces (170 to 184 g).

RUFFED GROUSE

Some hunters maintain that a ruffed grouse intentionally selects a flight path that places a tree directly in the line of fire. Whether intentional or not, the ruffed grouse is a difficult target for even the best wingshooters.

Grouse accelerate rapidly, reaching a speed of 40 mph (64 km/h) in seconds. But they seldom fly more than 200 yards (183 m). Grouse do not run as fast or as far as most other upland birds. When disturbed, birds of both sexes utter a call that sounds like pete-pete-pete.

Many hunters call the birds partridge, but the term is a misnomer. The only true partridge in North America are the chukar and Hungarian. The name ruffed grouse comes from the ruff, a tuft of dark feathers on the neck.

Hardwood forests with small clearings and mixed-age aspen trees make the best ruffed grouse habitat. Aspens provide good nesting cover and a year-round source of food. Grouse also favor birch trees, but also live in many other types of hardwood and conifer-hardwood forests.

Besides aspen buds, leaves and twigs, other foods include berries, fruits, clover, nuts, insects and occasionally corn. On warm, sunny days with little wind, grouse feed most of the morning and again in late afternoon. Cold, snowy or windy weather drives the birds into dense thickets or conifer stands. Grouse usually roost on the ground or in conifer trees, but when snow depth reaches 8 to 10 inches (20 to 25 cm), they often burrow into the snow.

Before the spring breeding season, male grouse begin drumming to advertise themselves to females. A bird stands on a log, braces his body with his tail, then starts beating his wings. The sound resembles that of a one-cylinder gasoline engine starting slowly, then gradually speeding up. Some drumming continues through summer and into fall.

Grouse nest in April or May, producing a brood of eight to ten chicks. By fall, the birds are full grown and the brood scatters. Young grouse usually move at least 1 mile (1.6 km) and some relocate up to 10 miles (16 km) from the hatching site. Once they establish territories, they move very little the rest of their lives.

Young birds lack the wariness of those that have been pursued by hunters. Often a young grouse will sit on the ground or on a tree limb in full view of a hunter. But the birds gain experience quickly. They learn to flush well ahead or from behind a tree or patch of dense brush where the hunter has difficulty seeing them. In remote areas, adult grouse are no more wary than young birds.

Throughout much of the northern regions, ruffed grouse populations are cyclical, peaking about every ten years. Populations in peak years may exceed those in poor years by a ratio of 15 to 1.

Ruffed grouse are some of the most available but under-hunted upland birds. With a range from northern California to Alaska and east to the Atlantic, public land birds are available to anyone with a full tank of gas and a shotgun.

Hunting for Ruffed Grouse

Every grouse hunter has been frustrated upon hearing a whirr of wings, scanning the dense cover, then spotting a bird just as it disappears from sight.

In early season, you may scare up a dozen grouse for every one you see in time for a shot. Even though the birds generally flush close by, leaves severely limit your range of vision. By the time the leaves fall, grouse have become spookier and tend to get up farther away. But they are much easier to see and seldom flush out of shooting range.

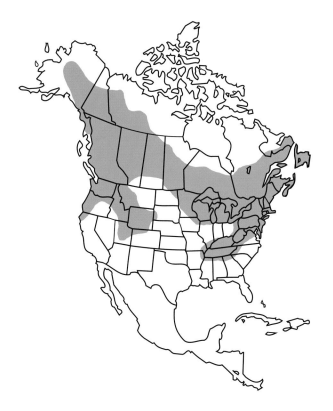

Ruffed grouse have a broad, black or dark brown band on the tail. The band is unbroken on most males, but broken on the center two feathers on females. There are two color phases, red and gray. Red-phase birds are more common in the South and at low altitudes; grays predominate in the North and at high altitudes. Grouse measure 17 to 20 inches (43 to 51 cm) long. They weigh 16 to 24 ounces (454 to 680 g), but occasionally reach 2 pounds (0.9 kg).

A good dog improves your grouse hunting success. But a dog is not essential because grouse are easier to flush than pheasants or quail. Most hunters prefer pointing breeds, but flushers and retrievers can also be effective if they work close to the handler. Because grouse are so well camouflaged, they can be difficult to find without a good dog.

When hunting without a dog, walk through likely cover and stop frequently. You can sometimes hear the birds nervously clucking before they fly. With two or more hunters, walk on opposite sides of thick patches. One hunter is likely to get a shot when a bird flushes.

If you miss or fail to get off a shot, watch where the bird lands. A flushed bird often flies off to a dense thicket or lands in a tree. You may be able to approach close enough for a second attempt.

You can improve your success by checking the crop of a freshly killed bird to find out what it was eating. Then, hunt where these foods are plentiful.

Grouse hunting is usually best on calm, sunny days. It seldom pays to hunt in early morning because the birds are still on their roosts. They begin moving after the woods have dried off.

A short-barreled, 20-gauge shotgun with an improved cylinder choke is an ideal grouse gun. The short barrel makes the gun easy to carry through heavy brush and enables you to swing quickly. Most grouse hunters prefer No. 7½ or 8 shot.

SIGNS OF GROUSE ACTIVITY

Tracks are closely spaced and about 2 inches (5 cm) long. A grouse places one foot directly in front of the other, so the tracks form a straight line.

Droppings on a drumming log mean that ruffed grouse are nearby. The brownish or greenish droppings are about ¼ inch (6 mm) in diameter.

Holes in the snow may be burrow-roosting sites. Burrows have an entrance hole and, if the bird has left, an exit hole.

Pointing dogs pin down grouse, enabling you to get close enough for an unobstructed shot. When you move in to flush the bird, avoid walking into dense cover where shooting would be difficult.

GROUSE HUNTING TECHNIQUES

Work the edges of cover. Grouse spend much of their time feeding on fruits and berries that grow along sunlit borders. If a bird flushes, your chances of getting a clear shot are better than in a thick woods.

Walk along a logging road, powerline cut or other trail through the woods. Trails make for easy walking and the edges produce food that attracts grouse. Try to avoid backtracking along the same path.

Listen for drumming ruffed grouse while hunting. Although most drumming activity takes place in the spring, some males continue to drum into the fall, revealing their locations to hunters.

TIPS FOR HUNTING RUFFED GROUSE

Plan your strategy using detailed maps of your hunting locale. State forestry departments may publish fire-control maps that show trails and logging roads.

Attach a bell to the collar of your pointing dog. This helps you keep track of its location. When the bell stops ringing, the dog is on point.

Scan the trees as you walk. Listen for a short flutter of wings that means a grouse has hopped up to a branch. Grouse in trees evidently feel safe, often allowing hunters to approach within gun range.

Other species are quicker to run or flush, but grouse hold tight while a hunter walks by. Its plumage blends so perfectly that you may never see the bird. That is until it flushes behind you.

SHARP-TAILED GROUSE

A novice hunter may mistake a sharptail for a hen pheasant, realizing the error only after the bird sails out of range. The two are about the same size and color, but a sharptail has a short, whitish tail and usually clucks when it flushes.

Sharptails prefer large ungrazed grasslands with numerous pockets of trees and brush for cover and fields of small grain for food. They favor wheat, oats and barley, but also eat berries, seeds, clover and buds. The birds feed in grain stubble or weed patches in early morning, loaf in wooded or brushy areas in midday, then feed again in late afternoon. Sharptails normally roost on the ground.

In early fall, a flock consists of six to eight birds. Later, many flocks combine to form a large pack which may have over 200 birds. When the birds flush, the flock stays together. They usually fly at least ½ mile (0.8 km) and occasionally a mile or more. But a bird or two may hold, so work the area thoroughly. Sharptails are strong runners and sometimes elude hunters by racing out the end of a field as the hunt begins.

Early-season hunters use 12- or 20-gauge shotguns with improved cylinder or modified chokes and No. 6 shot. After the birds form packs, they are harder to approach, so a full choke may work better.

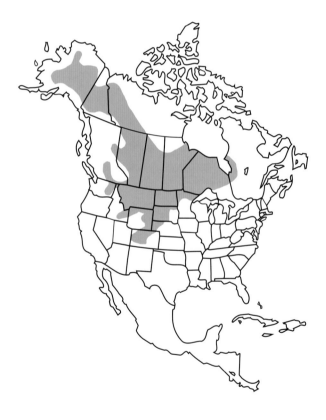

Sharptails are named for the two long feathers in the center of the tail. The brownish back and wings are covered with white spots. Males have a patch of yellow skin above each eye. These patches are less visible after the breeding season. The birds weigh up to 2 pounds (0.9 kg).

WHERE TO FIND SHARPTAILS

Look for sharptails in stubble fields early or late in the day. Carry binoculars to spot the birds and listen for clucking sounds.

Hunt along brushy ravines in windy or stormy weather. A ravine, grassy ditch or the lee side of a hill makes a good windbreak.

Check brush patches to find loafing sharptails. Other good loafing spots include shelterbelts and grassy areas around abandoned farms.

SAGE GROUSE

In the 1800s, up to 1.1 million sage grouse could be found in parts of what are now sixteen states and three provinces. Today, the sage grouse is a recluse, its population numbering around 160,000, found on sagebrush ground from Oregon through Wyoming and points north.

The birds inhabit open, semi-arid country with large sagebrush flats. Buds, leaves and shoots of sagebrush make up most of their diet. They also eat alfalfa, small grains, grasses, clover and berries. The birds feed along sagebrush edges in early morning. You can find them near water holes where they eat green vegetation. They rest in gullies and draws in midday, then feed again starting in mid-afternoon.

In early fall, birds may be found in groups of six to sixty, on open flats, plateaus, ditches and ridge tops.

Hunt the edges of agricultural land, where the fields meet the flats. For best success, hunt close to stock tanks and ponds. In dry times, grouse may fly in from long distances to get the moisture they crave.

To find sage grouse, glass from a ridge in early morning. Check open areas and edges of cover. If you spot birds, attempt a stalk. If not, identify water holes, sagebrush edges and ravines that you could hunt later. A pointing dog works well in early season. But when the birds start to run, a flusher or retriever is more effective.

At the flush, the birds come up in ones and twos, giving you the time to pick a target, swing with it and shoot.

Use a 12-gauge with a modified or full choke and No. 6 shot to down sage grouse. Some hunters shoot only smaller birds. The meat of older, larger birds tends to be tough and gamey.

Sage grouse have a mottled, grayish-brown back, a pale breast and flanks and a black belly. The long, pointed tail feathers fan out in flight. Males have a black patch on the chin and upper neck and a white V across the throat. Females are much smaller than males. The mature male sage grouse can weigh up to 7 pounds (3 kg) and stretch the tape to 30 inches (76 cm) from his beak to the tip of his tail.

WHERE TO FIND SAGE GROUSE

Hunt near stock tanks, ponds, irrigation ditches or creeks, especially in dry weather. These spots are best in early morning and just before dark. Sage grouse are seldom more than ½ mile (0.8 km) from water.

Rush a flock of sage grouse once you stalk within shooting range. They cannot get off the ground as quickly as other upland birds, so this tactic enables you to gain yardage for a closer shot.

CHUKAR PARTRIDGE

Chukar habitat is steep, dry, almost inaccessible and generally unsuitable for anything but wildlife. Much of the good hunting is on public land and access is generally not a problem. Chukars use rocky slopes for roosting and escape cover.

Named for its call, the chukar was imported from India in the late 1800s. Populations became established in arid portions of the Northwest. Typical chukar habitat varies from bare rocks to sparse grasslands. Because of the open country, the coveys are easy to see, but difficult to approach. They run uphill at the sight of a hunter. When they flush, they usually fly downhill.

Seeds, grasses, leaves, insects and fruit make up most of the chukar's diet. The coveys, which average ten to twenty birds, begin feeding in mid-morning. On cool days they may feed through the afternoon. They often cover over 1 mile (1.6 km) on their feeding rounds. In hot weather, chukars spend the middle of the day loafing in the shade of rocky bluffs or near springs and water holes. In windy or stormy weather, they seek depressions or crevices in the rocks.

Early in the season, when the weather is dry and hot, chukars will not be far from water. After fall's first rains, they may be more widely dispersed. Cheatgrass is one of the chukar's principal food sources, though the birds may also be found in agricultural areas close to the river and canyon habitat they prefer.

In summer and early fall, chukars can be found at altitudes up to 11,000 feet (3,353 m). A heavy snowfall will drive them to lower elevations.

A 12- or 20-gauge modified-choke shotgun makes a good chukar gun. Most hunters use No. 6 or 7½ shot.

Chukars have a grayish-brown back, a reddish bill and legs and a black collar that passes through the eye. Black and chestnut bars cover the flanks. Chukars average about 15 inches (38 cm) long and weigh 18 to 24 ounces (510 to 680 g).

HOW TO HUNT CHUKARS

Hunt with pointing dogs to help pin down the birds and prevent them from running. When your dog detects fresh scent, move into shooting position quickly because chukars may not hold to a point for long.

Follow chukar tracks after a fresh snowfall. In addition to providing good tracking conditions, snow makes the birds hold tighter and prevents them from running as fast as they do on bare ground.

HUNGARIAN PARTRIDGE

Hungarian partridge are birds of the wide open spaces and can be found in cropland, sage and bunchgrass country in Washington, Oregon, Nevada, Idaho, Montana, Wyoming and points east. Look for foothill habitat close to irrigated ag lands for the best hunting.

Huns have an understated beauty, with a form that follows function. Wings of white and mottled brown allow the bird to hide from predators by holding still. A pastel-gray on the breast blends on the head with shades of brown. Their eyes are surrounded by a pencil-thin border of red. Flanks and breasts are splotched with markings of chocolate brown.

Hunters find the birds in short, light cover. Huns feed mainly on grains like corn, oats, wheat and barley, but also eat weed seeds and green leaves.

Huns begin feeding after most of the dew dries off the grass. They feed until late morning, loaf in a grassy area until mid-afternoon, then resume feeding until dusk. The birds roost in alfalfa fields, grain stubble, short grass or even on plowed ground. They often form roosting rings like those of bobwhite quail. In winter, huns may roost in a depression in the snow or burrow-roost under it.

Coveys normally consist of ten to twelve birds. Huns do not hold well when first approached. They tend to sneak ahead of a hunter or dog, then burst from cover in unison. The covey remains together. Early in the season, huns fly only a short distance. As the season progresses, they go farther, sometimes over ½ mile (0.6 km).

Shotguns and shells used for huns are similar to those used for chukars. Some hunters prefer 12-gauge guns with full chokes in late season.

Huns are as spooky as chukar, faster than quail and smart enough to run, circle and hide. Add to all that its taste on the table and this import from Hungary is a welcome and worthy quarry for the best dogs and hunters.

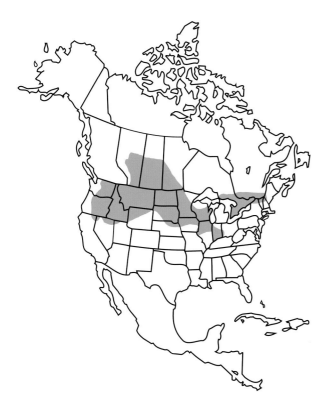

Hungarian partridge are technically named gray partridge. Native to Hungary, they have a cinnamon head and chestnut bars on the flanks. Males have a chestnut horseshoe on the breast. The birds weigh about 1 pound (0.45 kg) and measure 12 to 14 inches (31 to 35.5 cm) long.

HOW TO HUNT HUNGARIAN PARTRIDGE

Watch the covey land, then approach the spot from opposite sides. This prevents the birds from slipping away and assures someone of a shot. You can often flush the same covey again.

Hunt with a close-working retriever or flusher or use a pointing dog. Flushers and retrievers work best in high cover; wide-ranging pointers find more birds in sparse grasslands or other open terrain.

WILD TURKEY

Every year, hundreds of thousands of hunters head out in pursuit of a gobbler. Winter's weariness is receding with the snowline. Forests are coming to life. Fields of wildflowers are awash with the yellows, pinks and blues. There are spotted fawns in the thickets and new growth on the trees. To many hunters turkey hunting is a celebration of spring.

The wild turkey is the largest game bird in North America. It is found throughout North America (except for Alaska). Hawaii has an abundant (introduced) turkey population. There are five recognized subspecies, which vary slightly in color and size.

First-time turkey hunters may wonder if they could tell a male from a female. There are definite differences.

The male wild turkey, called a tom or gobbler, is a large, robust bird weighing up to 30 pounds (13.5 kg) and standing as high as 4 feet (1.2 m) tall. His body color is brownish black with a metallic, iridescent sheen. The head and neck, nearly bald, vary from white to blue to red. Bright red, fleshy bumps, called carbuncles, droop from the front and sides of the neck and a fleshy flap of skin, called a dewlap, is attached to the throat and neck. A fingerlike protrusion called a snood hangs over the front of the beak. When the tom is alert, the snood constricts and projects vertically as a fleshy bump at the top rear of the beak.

On the gobbler's breast there is a beard, a series of coarse hair-like fibers. On a jake, an immature gobbler, the beard may be only 3 inches (7.6 cm) long. A mature male has a beard approaching 8 inches (20 cm) in length and longer. This is not a feature totally exclusive to gobblers though, as some females may sport a beard.

Another feature that sets toms apart from hens is spurs. Hens have no spurs. Spurs are found on a gobbler's lower legs and average between ½ and 1½ inches (2.5 and 3.8 cm) long. These spurs are small and rounded on young birds; long, pointed and usually very sharp on mature birds.

Toms begin their breeding displays in early spring. With tail fanned, feathers fluffed, and wingtips dragging, the tom struts boldly while emitting low-pitched hums.

In the spring season, big gobblers are looking for love. This makes them vulnerable to hunters who can call a tom into range by imitating the varied calls of the hen. Several styles of turkey calls are available, making it easy for a hunter to find one that suits his hunting style and abilities.

The male is called a gobbler for good reason: his rattling, deep-toned call is one of the most recognizable sounds in all of nature. At mating time, toms gobble with full-volume gusto, attempting to attract hens for breeding. Adult males display for hens by fanning their tail feathers, puffing up their body feathers and dragging their wings as they strut. Their heads and necks turn bright red during breeding season or when the tom is otherwise excited.

Adult females, or hens, are considerably smaller than toms, rarely weighing more than 10 to 12 pounds (4.5 to 5.4 kg). Their overall body color is duller than the male's and lacks his metallic, iridescent sheen. The hen's head and neck are usually blue-gray in color and sparsely covered with small, dark feathers. Carbuncles are sometimes present, but smaller than those on toms. Some hens grow small, rudimentary beards and spurs. Although they don't gobble, hens make a variety of cluck, purr, cutt and yelp sounds. Dominant hens may assert themselves with a display resembling that of the male, though they do not strut.

Juvenile birds mature quickly. By their fifth month, the juvenile male (jake) and juvenile female (jenny) closely resemble adult birds. However, juveniles have darker legs, which turn pink as the birds age. Jakes make

feeble gobbles, higher in pitch than the calls of mature toms. Their beards are shorter in length and usually have amber-colored tips.

With its powerful legs, the wild turkey is an exceptional runner and has been clocked at speeds up to 12 mph (19 km/h). Although strong short-distance fliers, turkeys usually run when threatened. When necessary for escape, turkeys launch themselves with a standing leap or a running start and accelerate to 35 mph (56 km/h) in a matter of seconds. They cannot remain in the air for more than a few hundred yards (m), but can glide for ½ mile (0.8 km) or more when coasting down from a ridge top.

Subspecies

Subspecies can be difficult to distinguish from one another, since regional variations within the group can be more dramatic than physical differences between the subspecies. In addition, where the subspecies' ranges overlap, crossbreeding produces hybrid birds that show traits of both parents. A map showing the current range of all five subspecies is a good starting point in determining where subspecies live.

Turkey Calls and Decoys

Turkey calls have been an important part of the hunt ever since man discovered he could talk turkey and the birds would respond. Calls are deadly at drawing toms to hunters.

Calling is considered by most devoted turkey hunters to be the only sporting way to take a gobbler. Calling is the fun part of turkey hunting. Mastering a variety of different calls—learning when to yelp, cluck, purr or cutt, knowing when to call softly and when to crank up the volume—this is the art of spring turkey hunting.

Under the right circumstances, turkeys can be ridiculously easy to call. But don't count on it. When hens are abundant or hunting pressure is heavy, only a

Turkey calls can be divided into two basic categories: Friction calls include the (1) push-pull call, the (2) box call and the (3) slate-and-peg call. Air-activated calls include the (4) tube call and the (5) diaphragm call.

PROPER DIAPHRAGM CALL PLACEMENT

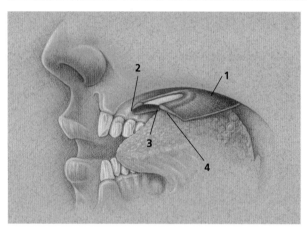

Proper placement of a diaphragm call in your mouth is crucial to success. (1) Use your tongue to position the call against the roof of your mouth with the straight edge facing forward. (2) Position the call so the forward edge nearly touches the back of your top front teeth. (3) Place the top of your tongue lightly against the latex reed and (4) expel short bursts of air between the top of your tongue and the reed, while saying the word "chirp." Stay at it and you will soon be able to produce acceptable yelps, the first call you should learn. Once you have mastered the yelp, begin practicing other calls.

CALLING TIPS

Insert a piece of cloth or fleece under the paddle, then wrap a rubber band around paddle and box. This keeps the call from squeaking as you walk.

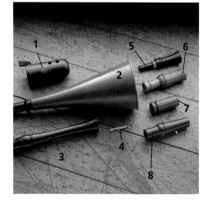

Dependable locator calls include: (1) owl hooter, (2) coyote howler with large bellows, (3) flute-style goose call, (4) silent whistle with adjustable frequency, (5) crow call, (6) pileated woodpecker call, (7) hawk screamer and (8) predator call.

Trim the skirt of a diaphragm call with small scissors to make it fit comfortably against the roof of your mouth.

Hen decoy styles include: (1) collapsible foam; (2) folding shell; (3) silhouette; (4) full body; (5) hen with safety orange head, which is both safe and often aggravates toms; and (6) motion decoy, which allows the hunter to move the head of the decoy by pulling on a long string.

Jake decoy styles include: collapsible foam in (1) full strut; (2) half-strut; and (3) erect position; and (4) folding shell in erect position.

hunter who has mastered the art of calling walks out of the woods with a gobbler slung over a shoulder.

Calls designed to lure gobblers to the hunter can be divided into two broad categories: friction calls and air-activated calls. Although each has its advantages and disadvantages, the friction calls are generally easier to operate.

A third category of calls, locator calls, are used to elicit a response from a turkey without attracting the bird to your position. This response is most commonly referred to as a shock gobble. Turkeys have been known to shock gobble to the sound of a squeaking fence, slamming car door or a bellowing Holstein and a host of other sudden, loud sounds. Most locator calls imitate animals such as crows, owls and coyotes, but loud cutting on a turkey call can also prompt a shock gobble.

There are dozens of commercial calls on the market and while there is no need to buy and use all of them, a hunter is wise to use a variety of calls. Wild turkeys can be fickle, preferring a box call one morning, a diaphragm the next. A well-prepared hunter is ready to switch calls on those mornings when his old standbys just aren't making the grade.

However, as important as calling is, woodsmanship is equally important. In fact, an accomplished woodsman—a hunter intimately familiar with the land

and the turkeys that live on it—can take gobblers with amazing consistency without ever touching a call.

A well-positioned turkey decoy is often the final touch needed to lure a shy tom into shooting range. Especially in open country, toms responding to a hen call may grow suspicious if they can't spot the source of the call. But if they see a decoy, the reassured gobblers often commit and waltz into range. A decoy can work wonders on hard-hunted birds, which tend to be leery of even the best calling.

Understanding Daily Patterns

At first light, as turkeys begin to awaken in their roosting trees, toms begin to gobble, while hens utter soft tree yelps. Usually the birds fly to the ground as soon as there is enough light for them to spot predators, but this fly-down can be as late as two hours after sunrise if the morning is rainy or foggy. Turkeys roosting in small woodlots in relatively open areas tend to fly down sooner than birds roosting in deep timber, where daylight is longer in arriving.

When a turkey gobbles on the roost in early morning, he is trying to draw a hen to him. If successful, the tom will fly down to join the hen. If a hen doesn't appear, the tom flies down and walks to his strutting area, while continuing to gobble.

To effectively hunt wild turkeys in spring, a hunter must understand the bird's daily movement patterns. Bagging a wild turkey is largely a matter of being in the right place at the right time.

Strutting zones are located in open areas where toms can be easily seen by hens, such as a field edge, logging road or pasture. In hill country, strutting areas are often located on elevated ridges, points or hilltops. In flat country, gobblers often strut in semi-open hardwood bottoms.

When the tom arrives at the strutting zone, he continues to gobble until he attracts a hen. Once a hen arrives, however, the gobbler begins to strut and his gobbling becomes infrequent. The tom may attract several hens simultaneously.

A gobbler follows hens as they wander to feed, mating with each several times during the morning, if they permit. Identifying feeding areas can be difficult, since wild turkeys eat such a wide variety of food. In big timber, turkeys often wander along, foraging on whatever they find. In agricultural areas, turkeys feed in crop fields a good deal of the time.

Only in the arid regions of the West and Southwest do turkeys habitually seek water during their daily route. In most regions they obtain sufficient water from dew or in the plants they consume.

By mid- to late morning, after satisfying their hunger, turkeys often treat themselves to a dust bath. Bred hens may then retire to the nest to lay or incubate. Gobblers may rest at this time or resume gobbling and continue to search for new hens.

Mid-afternoon finds turkeys on the move and feeding once again. During the last hour of day, the flock feeds toward roosting sites. They usually fly up at sunset or shortly thereafter. Birds often change limbs or even roosting trees a number of times before settling in for the night.

Turkey Hunting

One wrong move and the turkey will duck his head and run. Don't move a muscle, not yet. Let him close to 30 yards (27 m). He stops to strut, fanning out his tail feathers and puffing out his chest as if to say, "Look at me, ladies. Ain't I the pretty one, though?"

Ideally, you'll want to "roost" a gobbler on the eve of the hunt, which means you actually see or hear the bird in his roost tree. Return before first light, slip within 100 yards (91 m) of this roost, sound a couple of tree yelps at dawn and odds are good the gobbler will fly down practically in your lap.

To "put a bird to bed," set up near a roosting site in early evening. Turkeys feed toward a roost tree in late evening, usually fly into them around sunset and settle in before dark.

If you cannot spot birds, listen for them. Occasionally, toms gobble a time or two after roosting and hens sometimes yelp. More often, you'll have to make them gobble by using a locator call. Walk through likely habitat, pausing every ¼ mile (0.4 km) or so to call. If a gobbler responds, move toward him, eliciting additional shock gobbles until you've pinpointed his location. Mark the site and the trail to it with strips of toilet paper or surveyor's tape so you can find your way back before dawn.

As day breaks, give a few quiet tree yelps. Chances are good that the gobbler will reply, but if he doesn't, resist the temptation to call louder or more often. Overcalling while a tom is still on the roost is a common mistake.

If you failed to put a gobbler to bed the night before, plan to be at a good listening position well before first light. Hilltops and ridges are best. On most mornings, toms begin gobbling spontaneously, but if you hear no gobbling by the time there is enough light for you to see individual limbs on trees, then try to elicit a gobble with an owl or crow call. When you hear a gobbler within reasonable distance, try to get within 100 yards (91 m) before setting up to call him.

Turkeys usually fly from the roost as soon as there is enough light for them to see predators on the ground. However, on rainy, foggy or unseasonably cold mornings, they may stay on the roost for an hour or more after sunrise.

They use the same strutting grounds day after day. These are usually in relatively open areas, such as open timber, field edges, pastures or logging roads, where toms can watch for approaching hens and hens can clearly see their strutting displays. Once you find these sites, you can hunt them productively for years, because turkeys return to the same strutting zones season after season.

Hunters often make the mistake of yelping loudly and frequently. Call just enough to let a gobbler know you are there. Every few minutes, scratch the ground to mimic the sound of a foraging turkey. This assures the gobbler that a hen is still nearby, but since she ignores his calling, he sometimes goes against his own instinct and sashays toward her.

The prime early morning strutting/gobbling period may last a few minutes to an hour. Occasionally, a tom returns to his strutting zone in late morning after his original partners abandon him.

Two strategies can produce results after the prime early morning period: run-and-gun or sit-and-wait.

To use the run-and-gun approach, walk quickly through the area, stopping frequently to blow a locator call. Search for a bird that responds to every call you make. When you find such a bird, get within 200 yards (183 m) in open country, half that distance in timber; sit down and get ready before you make a single hen call. Call just often enough to keep the bird gobbling, so you know where he is. If the bird continues to gobble in response to your calls, but moves steadily away, determine his direction and attempt to get ahead of him. If he moves steadily in your direction, call sparingly and stay ready.

The sit-and-wait tactic is most successful if you know the area well enough to predict travel routes. Picking a good feeding spot and waiting patiently for a flock of hungry birds to arrive is also a good tactic before 10:00 a.m. A blind can be a real asset when playing this waiting game, as can a decoy or two. Patience is the key. Turkeys feed at midmorning and a feeding flock is in no hurry, covering only about 200 yards (183 m) per hour, on average.

Cover lots of territory after 10 a.m. Use locator calls and loud cutting to elicit gobbles. Locator calls are better than hen calls for prompting a tom to begin gobbling. Once you've elicited a shock gobble, set up and get ready to seduce the bird with your most authentic hen calls. If you begin by making hen yelps, a tom may arrive before you are prepared to deliver the proper greeting.

The first step in a successful hunt is to find good turkey habitat. Assuming you have scouted adequately, you should know several spots that hold birds.

If you prefer to sit and wait for your bird, late morning is a good time to stake out strutting zones. Gobblers that have been deserted by hens frequently meander back to their strutting zones and readily respond to calls.

Gobblers can still be taken in the afternoon, though it takes patience and a slightly different strategy. Find a turkey hangout—a dusting area or feeding site—set out a decoy or two, relax against a big tree and give a few yelps every 15 minutes or so. If a gobbler comes to your call at this hour, he usually won't announce himself until within shooting range. Many hunters have been jarred

from midday naps by tiptoeing gobblers shouting at close range.

Action picks up again in late afternoon, when turkeys begin actively feeding and, later, working toward the roost. If you have located a roosting area, determine the most likely direction from which the birds will approach and set up in their path. If you haven't pinpointed a roosting area, spend the last hour of daylight covering ground and using a locator call. If you hear a gobbler, slip in close and work the bird with hen calls. Even if you don't get a shot, you'll know where to continue the hunt in the morning.

HUNTING STRATEGIES

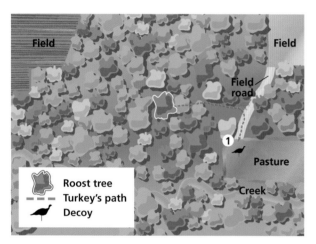

For typical early morning scenarios, set up in the nearest opening to the roost tree and put out a decoy. If the gobbler is alone, he will go to the field to gobble and strut. If he is with hens, he tags along as they go to feed in the field. The logging road is the obvious approach route.

For typical run-and-gun scenario image (top right):

If you want to set up a typical run-and-gun scenario, follow the easiest route to cover the most ground in the least amount of time when running and gunning. Skirt the edges of all openings and call every 100 to 200 yards (91 to 183 m), until you get a response.

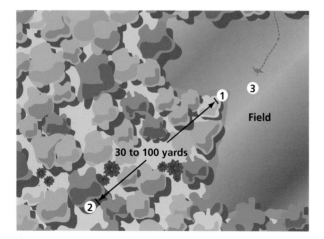

In a tag-team setup, position the shooter (1), 30 to 100 yards (27 to 91 m) in front of the caller (2). If a gobbler hangs up short of the caller, the bird will be within range of the shooter.

For a typical sit-and-wait scenario, sit and wait for birds where you can cover locations where birds enter or exit fields (1), pastures (2) or other openings. Be patient, call sparingly and stay alert.

MOURNING DOVE

It's hard to deny the thrill of seeing dozens of doves sweeping toward you and beyond, the sound of the wind in their wings. There's no more difficult wingshooting challenge than that you find on a dove hunt. These birds are hard to hit. You need an edge if you hope to bag enough for dinner.

North American hunters harvest about 50 million doves annually, more than all other migratory game birds combined. The continent's dove population is estimated at 500 million, making it the most common game bird.

Mourning doves don't like cold weather. In northern states, the birds begin flying south after the first frost. Prior to migration, they form flocks consisting of several hundred birds.

Doves prefer open fields with scattered trees and woodlots. The birds need water each day, so there must be a pond, stock tank, flooded gravel pit or river nearby. Doves nest in grass, shrubs, stubble fields or trees, especially evergreens.

Nesting begins in early spring and continues through early fall. Doves raise up to four broods, with both parents caring for the young. After predation and weather-related losses, broods average about one bird each. This trait of raising multiple broods is unique among game birds. It ensures a relatively stable population from year to year, with or without a hunting season.

Weed seeds form the bulk of the dove's diet. They favor foxtail, dove weed, ragweed and wild hemp. Other foods include corn, soybeans, sunflowers, oats and wheat.

Doves fly to their feeding areas at dawn, feed until mid-morning, then head for water. Through midday, they rest in dead or dying trees near a feeding area, a water hole or a small pond. Doves resume feeding in late afternoon, then return to a watering site late in the day.

At dusk, they fly to their roosts, often to the same trees they used during the day. If not disturbed, doves continue to use the same roosting and watering areas.

Mourning doves can fly up to 55 mph (88.5 km/h). Their normal flight is smooth, effortless and direct. But they flare quickly at the sight of hunters, darting and weaving erratically as they fly away.

Mourning doves have a slate-blue back, a fawn-colored breast with a pinkish cast and a black spot behind the ear. They measure 11 to 13 inches (28 to 33 cm) from head to tail and weigh about 3½ to 5 ounces (99 to 142 g).

Roosting trees are usually within 2 miles (3.2 km) of water. A favorite roosting spot is a sand bar in a river where the birds find dead trees close to water.

Hunting for Doves

Most dove hunters find a stand along a flight path. It may be a route between a roosting and feeding site or between a feeding and watering area. Conceal yourself in a brush patch or near a fence line or tree, then pass-shoot as the birds fly through.

Doves often fly near a dead tree, telephone pole or any object taller than the surrounding cover. They frequently fly through a gap in a tree line to reach a feeding area or water hole. Often they skirt the end of a point of cover extending into a feeding field. If stands within gun range of these spots do not produce, watch where the birds are flying and change your location accordingly.

By stationing several hunters around the edge, you can keep the birds moving and improve shooting for everyone.

Ideal habitat includes an old dead tree and muddy water with a bank free of brush. Scout for set-ups where a fencepost or a dead tree will break up your outline.

The best way to put birds in the game bag is to improve your shooting. Train to focus on one part of one bird. Key on a dove's beak for a passing shot or the tail feathers as it goes straight away. The tighter the focus, the better your chances are of bringing birds home for dinner.

That's difficult to remember in the heat of the action, but it is easily practiced on any bird you see. In time it becomes automatic.

There are more techniques to help the bird hunter fill the game bag. The first is timing. Take it slow. With an unloaded gun, practice disengaging the safety and shouldering it. The cheekpiece should come against your cheek, with the butt anchored against your shoulder. The barrel should be in the same plane as your master eye, front bead on (or ahead of) the target.

Picture the shot leaving the barrel in a string, similar to water in a hose. Imagine swinging a spray nozzle across the sky. When you swing your barrel, following through as you squeeze the trigger, your shot will "wash" the target in the same way.

A stool can improve your shooting. Lunging from a crouched position to shoot is awkward. Rising easily from a chair promotes good stance and shooting position.

Another essential is the earplug. There may be more shooting on one dove hunt than in all the rest of your season's bird hunts combined. Earplugs keep you from flinching, but more important, they protect the auditory organs. You want to keep your hearing sharp so, on opening day of dove season twenty years from now, you can still hear the whistle of the wind in their wings.

Camouflage clothing is ideal, but any drab outerwear will do. Many hunters use semi-automatic or pump shotguns. A variable or screw-in choke enables you to vary the shot pattern, depending on the range of the birds. An improved cylinder or modified choke with No. 7½ or 8 shot usually works best.

WHERE TO FIND DOVES

Water holes used by doves often have muddy water and bare ground along the edge. The best water holes have trees with dead branches nearby.

Idle fields attract doves because they provide an ample supply of weed seeds. Doves prefer to pick seeds from bare ground. They seldom feed in dense vegetation.

Gravel roads provide grit. Doves pick up sand and small gravel along roads in early morning and late afternoon. They also find grit along streams and in fields.

WOODCOCK

Woodcock have a chunky body with a mottled brownish back and sides and black bars on top of the head. They measure 10 to 12 inches (24.5 to 31 cm), weigh 6 to 8 ounces (170 to 227 g) and have a bill about 2½ inches (5 cm) long.

Eyes on the side of the head give the birds excellent lateral vision Some researchers believe that woodcock rely on an acute sense of hearing to find worms in the ground. The birds can fly as fast as 30 mph (48 km/h). When flushed, they usually land within 100 yards (91 m).

Most woodcock breed in the northern states and Canada. They start their southerly migration in early to mid-October, leaving en masse once the ground freezes or after a heavy snow. Woodcock stop off in the same resting areas each year.

Young forests with trees 10 to 20 feet (3 to 6 m) tall make the best woodcock habitat. The soil should be damp with little grassy cover. Heavy ground cover makes it difficult for the birds to find earthworms, their favorite food.

Woodcock feed mainly around dawn and dusk. Besides earthworms, the birds eat insect larvae, seeds, berries and green leaves. During the day, they rest on the ground, feeding only occasionally. In cool weather, look for them on sunny hillsides or other sunlit areas. On a hot day, they sit in the shade, often below evergreens.

The best woodcock hunting is during the migration period. Northern hunters may get some shooting at resident birds, but when the migration peaks, they may flush up to thirty birds per hour.

Hunters who use dogs flush a least twice as many birds as those who do not. Because woodcock blend so well with the leaves, downed birds can be difficult to find without a dog.

A short-barreled 20-gauge with an improved cylinder choke is an excellent gun for woodcock. Most hunters use No. 7½ or 8 shot, but some prefer No. 9.

Many hunters who own pointing dogs consider woodcock or timberdoodle, the ideal quarry. Even with a dog holding a close point, a bird will hold tight, confident in its near-perfect camouflage.

Chapter 7

HUNTING WATERFOWL

Waterfowl are ideally suited for a life spent in and around water. Webbed feet give them extraordinary swimming ability and their long necks and broad, flattened bills allow them to feed on aquatic plant and animal life. Waterproof plumage and thick layers of insulating down keep these birds from losing body heat in cold water.

Geese are distinguished by their large size, with some approaching 15 pounds (6.75 kg). During the migration, geese may form enormous flocks numbering in the tens of thousands. Geese exhibit no coloration differences between the sexes. They rarely breed before their second year and may live for twenty-five years. Geese mate for life and maintain stronger family bonds than do ducks, with both parents caring for the young.

Ducks differ from geese in that sexes usually vary in coloration. Males have distinctive, colorful plumage, while females are camouflaged with mottled, drab browns. Pair bonds are temporary, with the drake deserting the female shortly after breeding. Most ducks are short lived, but a few have been known to live fifteen years.

Puddle ducks include some of the most widely hunted species. Puddle ducks are adept at walking and feeding on land. They can take flight almost instantly by jumping straight into the air.

Diving ducks have legs and feet positioned far back on their bodies. Rather awkward on land, they spend most of their time in the water.

Identification for species and sexes requires a great deal of practice, especially with ducks. But you can recognize the major types of waterfowl by their body size and wingbeat. Geese are larger than ducks and their wingbeat is slower. Puddle ducks have a faster wingbeat, but not as fast as diving ducks.

WATERFOWL EQUIPMENT

Waterfowling requires more equipment than most other types of hunting. In many cases, you will need decoys, camouflage clothing, waders, binoculars, calls and a duck boat.

Regulations require hunters to use nontoxic shot. Most hunters prefer a 12-gauge with a modified choke for shooting ducks and geese, increasing the size of shot when hunting larger waterfowl such as geese.

Waterfowl hunters must think total concealment when setting up a decoy spread. Camouflage the hunter and the boat, and then utilize the proper call to "sell" the spread to incoming birds.

BASIC DUCK AND GOOSE CALLS

Duck Calls. *There are two basic types of mallard calls: standard, or Reelfoot, style and Arkansas style. Reelfoot calls have a metal reed that is curved upward at the tip. Arkansas calls have a straight plastic reed. Reelfoot calls are generally harder to blow and have a narrower range of tones, but are much louder. Consult an experienced local duck hunter to determine what kind of call works best in your area. The sound of a particular call may be more effective in one region than in another.*

Calls for other species include those for wood ducks, diver ducks and pintail-widgeon-teal whistle calls.

Goose Calls. *The basic types of goose calls include the standard call and the flute call. Standard goose calls are easy to blow. They create two tones, one low and one high pitch tone, that imitate the basic sound made by Canada geese. Low grunting feeder sounds can also be imitated using standard calls. Flute goose calls are more difficult to master, but can imitate the many different communication sounds of Canada geese. Callers use both hands to operate flute calls; one to hold the call while the other is cupped over the end of the call to regulate air flow.*

Calls for other species include those for white-fronted geese and snow geese.

Full-body floating decoys may be made of wood, cork, foam or molded plastic. A weighted or water-filled keel makes them float upright and a string and anchor keep them from drifting away. They come in standard and magnum sizes.

Field decoys: Shell decoys (bottom) are the most common among hunters because they are three-dimensional and can still be stacked for easy storage. Full-body decoys (top) add realism to your spread, but are probably the most bulky of all the styles. Silhouette decoys (middle) are very lightweight and easy to stack. Manufacturers now cut them in a wide variety of feeding, standing and resting positions, adding to the believability of the spread.

Decoy accessories include: (1) longline clip, for attaching decoy cords to longlines; (2) snap-swivels, which attach to decoy weights to prevent cord twist; decoy weights, such as (3) mushroom anchor, (4) pyramid anchor, (5) ring anchors, (6) strap anchor and (7) scoop anchor, which slips over the decoy's bill; (8) tangle-free decoy cord; (9) braided-nylon decoy cord; (10) decoy touch-up paint; and (11) grapple anchor for longlines.

Flagging devices attract the attention of waterfowl at a distance. Use a black or white flag for geese; a gray or black flag for ducks.

PUDDLE DUCKS

As their name suggests, these ducks commonly frequent small, shallow bodies of water, but they may also be found on big water. Also called dabblers, they feed on or just below the surface, mainly on aquatic vegetation. They may skim food off the water or they may tip up, submerging their upper body to feed while leaving their feet and rump pointing up. In fall, some puddle ducks also feed in grain fields. Their predominantly vegetable diet explains why they are considered better eating than most other ducks. Large wings give puddle ducks good maneuverability. They often circle a potential landing site several times, inspecting it closely before setting down. There are a total of twelve huntable puddle duck species in North America.

Puddle ducks are able to lift from the water almost instantly. They may be hunted by jump-shooting, pass-shooting, or by using decoys to draw them in.

HOW TO RECOGNIZE PUDDLE DUCKS

Tipping up or dabbling, is the usual puddle duck feeding method.

Colored wing patches are present on most puddlers. Most have a patch, called a speculum, on the wing's trailing edge. The speculum (arrow) is usually iridescent.

Legs positioned near the center of the body give a puddler good balance, so it can easily walk and feed on land.

Puddle-duck Hunting

The widespread distribution of puddle ducks, combined with their excellent table quality, accounts for their tremendous popularity among waterfowl hunters.

As a rule, puddle ducks prefer smaller water than diving ducks; even the shallowest slough or tiniest creek may offer top-rate hunting. But puddlers are also found on some of the continent's largest waters, including the Great Lakes and Utah's Great Salt Lake. While divers are comfortable riding out big waves in open water, puddlers are usually found in calm water. In windy weather, they seek shelter along a lee shore.

You don't need a lot of expensive equipment to hunt puddle ducks. Jump-shooting and pass-shooting require nothing more than a shotgun and a few shells and you can decoy the birds into a small body of water with only a half-dozen blocks. Hunting on big water, however, is much more involved and requires considerably more equipment, including a good-sized boat and a minimum of several dozen decoys.

Mallards are the most numerous of the puddle ducks and most other puddler species feel comfortable in their company. Teal, for instance, are commonly seen flying with mallards and wood ducks often loaf in the same area as mallards. As a result, you can use mallard decoys and calls to attract most any kind of puddle duck.

In setting decoys for puddle ducks, remember that puddlers rest in looser groups than divers, so your decoys can be spread out much more. Some hunters leave as much as 10 feet (3 m) between individual blocks. Diving-duck hunters seldom leave more than 6 feet (1.8 m).

Calling is of utmost importance in puddle-duck hunting. The birds, by nature, are quite vocal and they look for reassurance from ducks on the water before making the decision to land. If you are not a competent caller, however, it's better not to call; you'll scare away more birds than you'll attract.

Puddlers are generally considered to be smarter than divers, but this "intelligence" may, in part, be a reflection of their migration and feeding habits. Because they migrate earlier than divers, they're exposed to a longer period of hunting pressure, so they're more likely to recognize the difference between decoys and the real thing.

Float a small stream or river using a poke boat or a canoe. Hug the inside turns as long as possible. Ducks usually rest below the points and they won't see you coming until the last minute.

Use several goose decoys when hunting puddle ducks in the field. Ducks often feed with geese and the larger decoys add to the visibility of your spread.

Kick water with your boot when hunting flooded timber. The ripples indicate to circling ducks that others are dabbling in the water.

Pass-shoot from a strip of land between two lakes or between a lake and a grain field. Ducks choose the route that crosses the least land.

With the wind at hunters' backs, decoys should be set in two pods with a good-sized landing pocket between the pods. The outermost decoys should be no more than 30 yards (27 m) from the blind. The blind is positioned so the hunters are facing the pocket. Without a pocket, ducks may land beyond the decoys, out of shooting range.

With the wind from the left, arrange the decoys in a "C" formation to the left of the blind, as shown. Ducks do not like flying over decoys to land; this way, they do not have to. When the wind is from the right, reverse the entire decoy setup.

DIVING DUCKS

With legs positioned farther back on the body, these ducks are more adept at diving beneath the surface than are puddle ducks. Their feet are larger for their size, so they are better underwater swimmers. The leg position also makes it more difficult for them to walk on land, explaining why they seldom feed in agricultural fields. The diet of most divers consists mainly of invertebrates and fish, explaining their strong taste. But some, such as canvasbacks and redheads, feed heavily on wild celery and other aquatic vegetation and are considered better eating. There are nineteen huntable diving duck species in North America.

Sea ducks, a subcategory of diving duck, differ from ordinary divers in that they spend most of their life in coastal areas. They have remarkable diving ability, with some species descending to depths of more than 200 feet (61 m) to feed on mollusks, crustaceans and fish.

Mergansers, often called fish ducks, are also classified as a subcategory of diving duck. They feed even more heavily on fish than other divers and their serrated bill is ideal for catching and holding small fish until they can be swallowed whole. Their crested head easily distinguishes them from other diving ducks.

Diving ducks plunge well beneath the surface to feed.

HOW TO RECOGNIZE DIVING DUCKS

Large feet and legs positioned far back on the body account for the diving ability of these ducks. White to dark gray wing patches are found on most diving duck species.

Flying low over the water in tight flocks is typical behavior among most diver species. In flight, divers can be distinguished from puddlers by their shorter, faster wingbeat. Running on the water helps divers gain enough speed for take-off. Their small wings provide less lift than those of puddlers.

The pursuit of diving ducks takes hunters to broad rivers, estuaries, and in and around large saltwater bays. Strong fliers, they are one of waterfowling's greatest challenges.

Diving-duck Hunting

If you're looking for a wingshooting challenge, diving ducks are the perfect quarry. When a flock of divers streaks along a decoy line, it's not uncommon for a hunter to shoot at the lead bird and drop the third or fourth one back.

Due to the divers' preference for big water, hunters need more and different equipment than they ordinarily do for puddle-duck hunting. Instead of a 12- or 14-foot (3.7 to 4.3 m), shallow-draft duck boat, for instance, you'll need a 16- or 18-foot (5 to 5.5 m), deep-hulled semi-V to negotiate water that can turn rough in a hurry. You'll also need more decoys than you would for puddle-duck hunting and, possibly, a floating blind.

The divers' habit of forming large open-water rafts, particularly in late season, adds to the hunting challenge. Some hunters use low-profile sneak or sculling boats to approach birds in open water without alarming them.

Because divers migrate much later in the season than puddle ducks, you'll be hunting in considerably colder weather. Warm, waterproof clothing, including insulated boots and gloves, is a requirement.

Crippled divers often attempt to escape by swimming away underwater or with their head at water level. You'll need a determined, hardy retriever, preferably a Labrador or Chesapeake, that is capable of making long retrieves in cold, choppy water.

In puddle-duck hunting, the idea is to lure birds into the decoys and take them when they're "putting on the brakes," meaning that their wings are cupped and they are about to land. In diver hunting, the birds are less likely to slow down, so you'll probably have to take them as they're winging along a line of decoys that leads to your blind.

Instead of shooting at birds that are barely moving, you're attempting to hit birds barreling along at speeds up to 75 mph (120 km/h). To be successful, you must learn the swing-through shooting technique and do a lot of practicing to determine the proper lead.

Calling is seldom necessary in diver hunting. The birds spot the decoys from a distance and their curiosity draws them in without any vocal enticement. Nevertheless, many hunters try calling anyway, using a diver call or rolling their tongue against a mallard call to mimic the characteristic diver "purr."

Divers differ from puddlers in that they do not hesitate to land in rough water. As a result, there is no need to set your decoys off a lee shore. It's more important to set them where the birds are feeding, regardless of wind direction.

Yet another difference: divers do most all of their feeding on the water, so the field-hunting techniques that work so well for puddle ducks are not effective for divers. Practically all diver hunting is done on the water or on passes between two bodies of water.

Diver hunting is not for everyone. Not only does it require a high tolerance for inclement weather, it can be a lot of work. But if you're a hardy soul who loves the whistle of wings, there's no more exciting shooting.

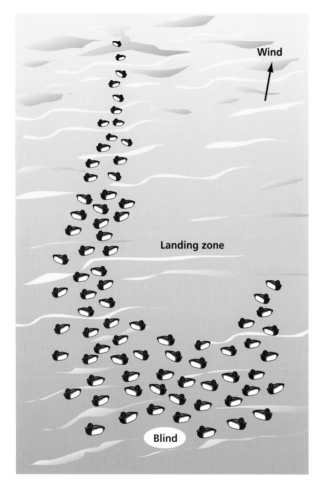

The J-hook. This setup works well off a point or in open water. The long tail extends well beyond shooting range. The largest clump of decoys is placed at the hook of the J, which forms a landing zone.

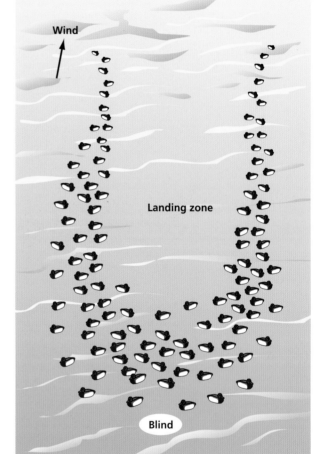

The V-formation. This setup is similar to the J-hook, but it has two tails extending out into the water, rather than one, giving the birds an additional option for approaching the blind.

DIVING-DUCK HUNTING TIPS

Use silhouette sleds, which can be neatly stacked so they take up less space than ordinary decoys. Attach the sleds to longlines; each should be rigged with about twelve sleds. Tie a full-body floating decoy to each end of the line to help keep the silhouettes afloat in rough water.

Make inexpensive diver decoys by painting black patches on white bleach jugs.

Low-profile boats allow you to get close enough for a good shot on diving ducks that have rafted up on the water.

Wave a black flag when you spot distant ducks. The motion resembles other ducks flying or landing. Stop flagging once the ducks start to head your way.

Look for openings in the trees or long points that extend out into the main body of water to pass-shoot divers.

GEESE

Geese often fly in a very distinct V-formation with a much slower wingbeat than ducks. Large, powerful wings enable geese to take flight very quickly, even though some Canada geese reach a weight of 15 pounds (6.75 kg). Once in flight, geese are easily recognized by their slower wingbeat when compared to the fast wingbeat of ducks.

Flocks consist of one or two family units, each numbering between four and six birds. As the migration progresses, many flocks join to form large concentrations, which may number in the thousands.

An exceptional homing instinct draws geese to the same waters every year. And they often return to the same feeding areas on consecutive days. If the food supply holds up, they come back to the exact spot in the field.

The fall diet of geese consists of waste grain, green plants such as clover, grasses and new shoots of barley, wheat and oats. Geese feed in open fields where they can see in all directions.

About three out of four bagged geese are juveniles, but some live twenty-five years. To survive that long, they must learn to be extremely cautious. Old birds scrutinize a landing site and veer off immediately if anything looks suspicious.

Dry land goose hunting is one of waterfowling's greatest thrills. The birds are big, with a wingspan of up to 71 inches (180 cm). The birds breed in Canada and the northern United States, then travel south in the fall in long Vs. They can be enticed with large decoy sets and calling.

Canada geese have a black head with a white chin bar. The back is grayish or brownish and the belly is whitish. Biologists recognize more than 12 varieties of Canada geese, the largest being the giant Canada; the smallest, the cackling goose.

White-fronted geese, also called speckle bellies, have a brownish head, neck and back. The undersides are whitish with dark brown speckles. A distinctive white facial patch rings the base of the pinkish bill.

Snow geese are pure white with black wing tips. Two subspecies are recognized: the greater snow goose and the lesser snow goose. Lesser snow geese may sport either dark or white plumage.

Ross geese resemble the lesser snow goose, but are smaller and have a stubbier bill. Ross geese often travel with snow geese and can easily be identified in flight by their faster wingbeat.

Brant geese, both Atlantic (bottom) and Pacific (top), can be recognized in flight by their rapid wingbeat. The head, neck and chest are black and the sides of the neck are marked with white streaks. The Pacific brant has a darker underside and more pronounced neck marks.

Hunting Geese

Those minutes before first light, the barley bending with the wind, the cool of the morning and the whispered anticipation of honking geese against a paling sky—this is what brings goose hunters to the field each year. That and the thrill of seeing the birds over the barrel of a gun, ten feet off the ground, their wings cupped to land.

Scouting, prior to the hunt, is essential. Note what time birds are seen in which fields and be there with your decoys the next day. Large flocks of strategically-placed plastic impostors, with good calling, will bring geese into shotgun range.

Hunting with decoys can be done both in feeding fields and on the water. When hunting in a field, you often need a large number of decoys to entice the birds.

When hunting for Canada or white-fronted geese in the early season, set your decoys in small clusters to imitate a small family group. Fewer decoys are often required early in the season because the geese haven't grouped up for the fall migration.

When hunting snow or Ross geese, some hunters use well over a thousand decoys in order to successfully decoy the most cautious waterfowl of North America. Combining large shell decoys and silhouette decoys, hunters mix in Texas Rag style decoys, white garbage bags and wind sock style decoys to increase the mass and visibility of the spread. Hunters rarely hunt snows on the water with decoys.

Brants can also be hunted with decoys, most commonly on the water. Setting two separate groups of decoys and leaving a place for the geese to land in the middle is the most common setup.

Most pass-shooting takes place in areas surrounding goose refuges or other waters with large concentrations of birds. Flight paths to and from a lake vary, depending on wind direction and the location of the feeding field being used. To select a good pass-shooting spot, spend a few hours watching the birds, taking note of the direction of the wind.

Hunters usually stalk geese after following or spotting a flock during their feeding period, which usually occurs twice daily, once in midmorning and again toward late afternoon.

Be prepared to use any available cover to sneak on a flock of geese. Sometimes they land in a field that is impossible to sneak. Better to find another flock where you are more likely to make a successful stalk.

When geese land in an open field, try team hunting. One hunter hides along an edge of the field, while another approaches from the opposite side. When the birds fly, they may pass over the hiding hunter.

Hunters accustomed to shooting ducks often have trouble hitting geese. Because the birds are so large, the tendency is to underestimate their distance and speed. Goose hunters use 12- or 10-gauge shotguns with modified or full chokes. Shot sizes range from No. 3 to T shot.

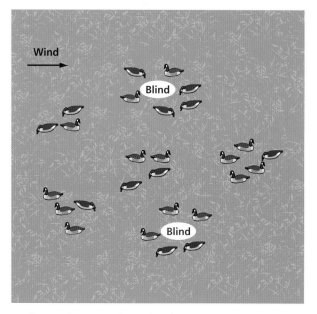

Family spread. Set Canada or white-fronted goose decoys in small family groups when hunting early in the season. Groups consist of four to ten decoys spaced about 5 to 10 yards (0.9 to 9 m) from each group. Set your blind(s) on the downwind side, shooting geese as they approach your spread.

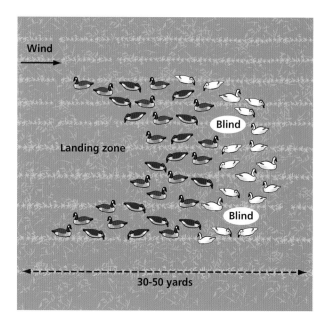

Combination field. Place snow goose decoys on the downwind side of the spread. On the upwind side, set your Canada decoys, leaving a large opening. Hide among the snow goose decoys or in a pit blind near the downwind side of the spread and shoot as the geese approach the landing zone from the downwind side.

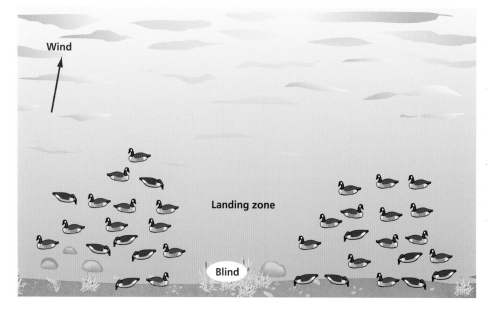

Water spread. Place your decoys in the most protected area of the bay, leaving an opening about 15 yards (13 m) wide for the birds to land in the middle of the spread. The opening should be directly in front of the blind. The outermost decoys should be no more than 35 yards (32 m) from the blind, giving you a distance guide to approaching geese. Depending on the size of the water you're hunting, you'll need from one to six dozen decoys to hunt geese on the water.

HOW TO USE A SHORT REED CALL

The Short Reed Goose Call provides the most versatile range of tone and pitch of any call on the market. Today, many variations are available, made from ABS, polycarbonate and acrylic. Calls made from ABS range are the least expensive. Polycarbonate calls are more expensive. Acrylics may be the most expensive, but they have the crispest tones.

The grip is critical. To create back pressure, put your index finger at the base of your thumb to form an O at the very end of the call. Then close your pinky finger and your ring finger against your palm as if in a fist. You use your middle finger to regulate the air pressure and flow to create all the sounds.

Play the call like you would play an instrument. Don't blow with your mouth. Air pressure should originate in your diaphragm.

Use your middle finger to change tones and your off-hand to direct the sound up and down and left and right. Begin to muffle the call as the birds get closer. The subtle sound keeps them coming.

Most goose hunters use a blend of several types of decoys. Here, the hunters are setting up shells. Flags and silhouettes are handy because they take up less storage space and can add depth to a spread.

Outfitter Darren Roe demonstrates proper calling form (right), employing a Basin Abomination short reed goose call. Use your middle finger to change tones and your off-hand to direct the sound up and down, left and right. Begin to muffle the call as the birds get closer. The subtle sound keeps them coming.

GOOSE HUNTING TIPS

Locate geese midmorning or late afternoon by scouting grain fields near resting waters. Secure permission and hunt the field the next feeding period.

Use flags to gain the attention of distant geese. The waving flags imitate geese fluttering in to a flock of feeding geese.

Pass-shoot geese flying to and from feeding areas. Many refuges allow hunting along the boundaries.

INDEX

PHOTO CREDITS

Note: T = Top, B = Bottom, C = Center, L = left, R = Right, I = inset

© Grady Allen: pp. 101, 116BR

© Charles Alsheimer: p. 63TR

© Erwin Bauer: pp. 8R, 26, 61C, 61CR, 61BL, 76B, 83T, 123BR

© Craig Blacklock: p. 58

© Les Blacklock: p. 12

© Tom Brakefield: p. 61T, Back Cover TL

© The Browning Company: pp. 48C, 149

© Glenn D. Chambers: p. 114

© Tim Christie: p. 93I, Front Cover BC

© Herbert Clarke: pp. 117, 119

© Daniel J. Cox: p. 16, 61 far left

© John Ebeling: p. 11BC

© John Ford: Front Cover T

© Michael Francis: pp. 99B, 104, Front Cover TC

© Michael Furtman: pp. 138, 146T

© Eric J. Hansen: pp. 6, 20, 44, 62, 71

© istock photo: p. 100

© Larry D. Jones: pp. 75BC, 75BR

© Gary Kramer: pp. 72, 73R, 85TL, 86, 105BL, 122, 128, 133, 142BR

© Lon E. Lauber: pp. 35, 39T, 65T, 66, 73L, 84, 92, 105BR, 129, 132

© Gary Lewis: pp. 85TR, 85B, 153R

© Tom Mangelson: pp. 54, 109TR

© Bill Marchel: pp. 142BL, 142CR, 150T, 150BL, 150BR, Front Cover B

© Tom Martinson: p. 8L

© Jay Massey: p. 50

© Worth Mathewson: p. 94

© Bill McRae: pp. 77BR, 81TL, 109TL

© Wyman Meinzer: p. 120

© Arthur Morris/Birds as Art: pp. 151TR, 151BR

© William H. Mullins: p. 124

© Doug Murphy: p. 11TL

© Nebraska Game And Parks Commission, 13

© Scott Nielsen: p. 142T, 146BL, 146BR

© Jerome B. Robinson: p. 55

© Lynn Rogers: p. 93T

© Leonard Lee Rue III: pp. 47CR, 63TL, 89T, 102T, 135

© Dwight R. Schuh: p. 77T

© Ron Shade: pp. 69, 75T

© Jerry Smith: p. 61BR

© Dale C. Spartas: pp. 11TR, 123T, 123BL

© Ron Spomer: pp. 10TR, 11BL, 11BR, 19BL, 95, 151L

© Norm Strung: p. 65B

© Syl Strung: p. 79BR

© Ken Thommes: pp. 99T, 105TL, 105TR, Back Cover BR

© Charles Waterman: p. 125

© Chuck Wechsler: pp. 61CR, 61 far right

© Ron Winch: p. 79T

© James Zacks: p. 10TL

© Gary Zahm: pp. 10BR, 118, 136

Creative Publishing international
Your Complete Source of How-to Information for the Outdoors

Hunting Books

* Advanced Turkey Hunting
* Advanced Whitetail Hunting
* Beginner's Guide to Birdwatching
* Black Bear Hunting
* Bowhunting Equipment & Skills
* Bowhunter's Guide to Accurate Shooting
* The Complete Guide to Hunting
* Dog Training
* Elk Hunting
* How to Think Like a Survivor
* Hunting Record-Book Bucks
* Mule Deer Hunting
* Muzzleloading
* Outdoor Guide to Using Your GPS
* Waterfowl Hunting
* Whitetail Addicts Manual
* Whitetail Hunting
* Whitetail Techniques & Tactics
* Wild Turkey

Fishing Books

* Advanced Bass Fishing
* The Art of Freshwater Fishing
* The Complete Guide to Freshwater Fishing
* Fishing for Catfish
* Fishing Tips & Tricks
* Fishing with Artificial Lures
* Inshore Salt Water Fishing
* Kids Gone Campin'
* Kids Gone Fishin'
* Kids Gone Paddlin'
* Largemouth Bass
* Live Bait Fishing
* Modern Methods of Ice Fishing
* Northern Pike & Muskie
* Panfish
* Salt Water Fishing Tactics
* Smallmouth Bass
* Striped Bass Fishing: Salt Water Strategies
* Successful Walleye Fishing
* Ultralight Fishing

Fly Fishing Books

* The Art of Fly Tying + CD-ROM
* Complete Photo Guide to Fly Fishing
* Complete Photo Guide to Fly Tying
* Fishing Dry Flies
* Fly-Fishing Equipment & Skills
* Fly Fishing for Beginners
* Fly Fishing for Trout in Streams
* Fly-Tying Techniques & Patterns

Cookbooks

* All-Time Favorite Game Bird Recipes
* America's Favorite Fish Recipes
* America's Favorite Wild Game Recipes
* Backyard Grilling
* Cooking Wild in Kate's Kitchen
* Dressing & Cooking Wild Game
* The New Cleaning & Cooking Fish
* Preparing Fish & Wild Game
* The Saltwater Cookbook
* Venison Cookery
* The Wild Butcher
* The Wild Fish Cookbook
* The Wild Game Cookbook

To purchase these or other Creative Publishing international titles,
contact your local bookseller, or visit our website at
www.creativepub.com